Linux Mint System Administration Beginner's Guide

A practical guide to learn basic concepts, techniques, and tools to become a Linux Mint system administrator

Arturo Fernandez Montoro

BIRMINGHAM - MUMBAI

Linux Mint System Administration Beginner's Guide

First published: December 2012

Production Reference: 2220213

Published by Packt Publishing Ltd.
Livery Place
35 Livery Street
Birmingham B3 2PB, UK

ISBN 978-1-84951-960-1

www.packtpub.com

Cover Image by Asher Wishkerman (wishkerman@hotmail.com)

Credits

Author
Arturo Fernandez Montoro

Reviewers
Antonio Hernández Díaz
Dennis Schwertel

Acquisition Editor
Sarah Cullington

Commissioning Editor
Ameya Sawant

Technical Editors
Vrinda Amberkar
Dennis John
Dominic Pereira

Copy Editors
Insiya Morbiwala
Aditya Nair
Laxmi Subramanian

Project Coordinator
Esha Thakker

Proofreader
Aaron Nash

Indexer
Hemangini Bari

Graphics
Melwyn D'sa

Production Coordinators
Melwyn D'sa
Manu Joseph

Cover Work
Melwyn D'sa

About the Author

Arturo Fernandez Montoro is a Software Architect specializing in design, development, testing, and deployment of high-traffic web applications.

Since 2002, he has been writing on Linux and Open Source technologies for different printed and online magazines, such as Todo Linux, Linux+, Linux Magazine, and Free Software Magazine. Also, he has authored *iPhone JavaScript Cookbook* for Packt Publishing.

His professional experience includes working in technologies, such as Django, Ruby on Rails, J2EE, PHP, web application servers, relational and NoSQL databases, JavaScript, HTML5, and CSS. He has spent the last 3 years working as a Software Architect and Python/Django Lead Developer.

Currently, Arturo lives in Madrid working as a Software Architect for QDQ Media, one of the biggest online marketing agencies in Spain. He can be reached at `arturo@bsnux.com`.

A very big thanks to the Linux Mint developers for developing one of the most amazing GNU/Linux distributions in the world. Millions of users enjoy Mint every day. Thanks for making my daily job easier.

Many thanks to my parents, who've always supported me in difficult times. They taught me to never give up.

Finally, I really appreciate all the work done by the team at Packt Publishing; thanks a lot for helping me publish this book.

About the Reviewers

Antonio Hernández Díaz is an active believer in Open Source from Seville, Spain. He has more than 10 years of experience working for IT companies, and although he is a web development expert, he has always known how to deal with other kinds of projects or technologies, such as desktop applications, mobile projects, or optimizing databases.

Since 2011, he has been involved in the development of various GNU/Linux distributions, either as a member of the Guadalinex development team (an Andalusian regional distribution), contributing humbly with Linux Mint, or just learning how to make Arch Linux ISOs in his free time.

When he is not working on some of his projects, it's not strange to see him on top of a kayak.

Dennis Schwertel is a software developer from Germany with many years of experience in working with Linux systems and developing desktops and large-scale web applications for international companies.

www.PacktPub.com

Support files, eBooks, discount offers and more

You might want to visit www.PacktPub.com for support files and downloads related to your book.

Did you know that Packt offers eBook versions of every book published, with PDF and ePub files available? You can upgrade to the eBook version at www.PacktPub.com and as a print book customer, you are entitled to a discount on the eBook copy. Get in touch with us at service@packtpub.com for more details.

At www.PacktPub.com, you can also read a collection of free technical articles, sign up for a range of free newsletters and receive exclusive discounts and offers on Packt books and eBooks.

http://PacktLib.PacktPub.com

Do you need instant solutions to your IT questions? PacktLib is Packt's online digital book library. Here, you can access, read and search across Packt's entire library of books.

Why Subscribe?

- Fully searchable across every book published by Packt
- Copy and paste, print and bookmark content
- On demand and accessible via web browser

Free Access for Packt account holders

If you have an account with Packt at www.PacktPub.com, you can use this to access PacktLib today and view nine entirely free books. Simply use your login credentials for immediate access.

I want to dedicate this book to those who think that my ideas and projects will never come true.

Table of Contents

Preface

In the last 5 years, the number of users for Linux-based operating systems has significantly increased. Many computer users want to know more about Linux, and a lot of them are migrating from other systems such as Windows and Mac OS X. Currently, Linux Mint is one of the most used Linux-based operating system, and many users want to improve their abilities to perform advanced tasks with this operating system. These include connecting to other computers through FTP, creating shell scripts, and organizing users into groups.

Linux Mint System Administration Beginner's Guide offers a set of practical recipes to become a Linux system administrator. With this book, you'll learn the basic concepts and operations that a Linux system administrator needs to know and perform. We'll start from the basic operations such as installing Linux Mint, and continue progressively learning more advanced topics such as security and monitoring.

Despite the fact that we're going to work with Linux Mint, most of the concepts and actions described by this book can be applied to other Linux distributions such as Ubuntu, Debian, and Fedora.

What this book covers

Chapter 1, Introduction to Linux Mint, is the "getting started" chapter of this book. It explains what Linux Mint is, what kind of editions exist, and why Linux Mint is different than other Linux distributions.

Chapter 2, Installing Linux Mint, teaches you how to install Linux Mint on your computer. It offers a simple and easy-to-follow, step-by-step guide for installing and booting this operating system.

Chapter 3, Basic Shell, introduces you to Linux shell. You'll learn how to deal with basic operations and actions such as finding out the current directory, setting the environment variables, and creating simple shell scripts.

Chapter 4, Account Provisioning, covers all you need to operate with user accounts, including how to create users and groups, and how to change the users' privileges.

Chapter 5, Installing, Removing, and Upgrading Software, teaches you how to carry out the basic actions to get the software working on your computer.

Chapter 6, Configuring Hardware, provides coverage of the process for detecting and configuring hardware devices, such as a keyboard, a mouse, a monitor, and a sound card.

Chapter 7, Networking, focuses on wired and wireless networks. You'll learn to configure your network and connect to other servers using the FTP protocol.

Chapter 8, Storage and Backup, covers different filesystem types. It teaches you to find out how much space your disk is using, and how to create and restore backups of your important data.

Chapter 9, Security, explores fundamental concepts you should know to run a secure Linux Mint computer. This chapter includes steps for installing and configuring a firewall, using a security module for the kernel, and explains how to build a simple and effective security checklist.

Chapter 10, Monitoring Your System, covers the main aspects of operating system monitoring. You'll learn about taking care of services and processes running on your computer, and how memory, CPU, and network are used.

Chapter 11, Troubleshooting, helps you to identify problems checking your hardware, networking, kernel, processes, and filesystems.

What you need for this book

Obviously, you need an Intel-based computer. Most computers, including laptops and desktops belong to this category. In order to install Linux Mint, you'll need a USB pen drive with at least 1 GB of capacity. Also, it's recommended to have a broadband Internet connection for downloading, installing, and upgrading the software.

Who this book is for

This book is for those computer users who are interested in learning about Linux system administration. You should be familiar with Linux-based operating systems and basic concepts such as directories, files, commands, and processes. Users who have experimented with Linux as well as *power users* can improve their knowledge for becoming system administrators.

Conventions

In this book, you will find several headings appearing frequently.

To give clear instructions of how to complete a procedure or task, we use:

Time for action – heading

1. Action 1
2. Action 2
3. Action 3

Instructions often need some extra explanation so that they make sense, so they are followed with:

What just happened?

This heading explains the working of tasks or instructions that you have just completed.

You will also find some other learning aids in the book, including:

Have a go hero – heading

These practical challenges and give you ideas for experimenting with what you have learned.

You will also find a number of styles of text that distinguish between different kinds of information. Here are some examples of these styles, and an explanation of their meaning.

Code words in text are shown as follows: "Save the ISO image, `linuxmint-13-mate-dvd-32b.iso` into your hard drive."

Any command-line input or output is written as follows:

```
arturo@han-solo ~ $ cd /tmp
```

New terms and **important words** are shown in bold. Words that you see on the screen, in menus or dialog boxes for example, appear in the text like this: "Click on the **Diskimage** option and select the downloaded ISO image using the button with the label".

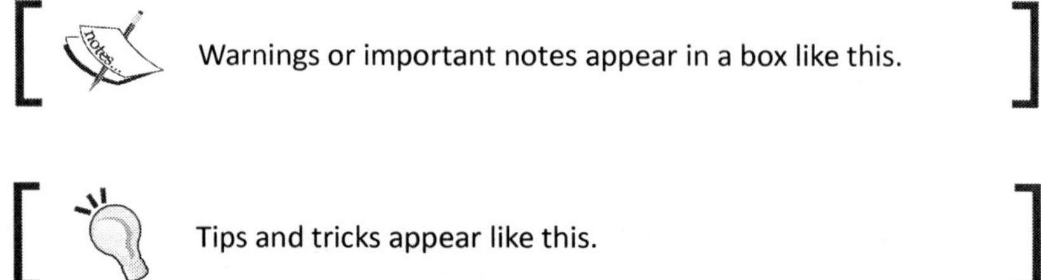

Reader feedback

Feedback from our readers is always welcome. Let us know what you think about this book—what you liked or may have disliked. Reader feedback is important for us to develop titles that you really get the most out of.

To send us general feedback, simply send an e-mail to `feedback@packtpub.com`, and mention the book title through the subject of your message.

If there is a topic that you have expertise in and you are interested in either writing or contributing to a book, see our author guide on `www.packtpub.com/authors`.

Customer support

Now that you are the proud owner of a Packt book, we have a number of things to help you to get the most from your purchase.

Errata

Although we have taken every care to ensure the accuracy of our content, mistakes do happen. If you find a mistake in one of our books—maybe a mistake in the text or the code—we would be grateful if you would report this to us. By doing so, you can save other readers from frustration and help us improve subsequent versions of this book. If you find any errata, please report them by visiting `http://www.packtpub.com/support`, selecting your book, clicking on the **errata submission form** link, and entering the details of your errata. Once your errata are verified, your submission will be accepted and the errata will be uploaded to our website, or added to any list of existing errata, under the Errata section of that title.

Piracy

Piracy of copyright material on the Internet is an ongoing problem across all media. At Packt, we take the protection of our copyright and licenses very seriously. If you come across any illegal copies of our works, in any form, on the Internet, please provide us with the location address or website name immediately so that we can pursue a remedy.

Please contact us at `copyright@packtpub.com` with a link to the suspected pirated material.

We appreciate your help in protecting our authors, and our ability to bring you valuable content.

Questions

You can contact us at `questions@packtpub.com` if you are having a problem with any aspect of the book, and we will do our best to address it.

1

Introduction to Linux Mint

Welcome to Linux Mint! It's time to discover one of the most amazing operating systems in the World. Linux Mint is not just an operating system. It's a complete open source project supported by hundreds of volunteers.

In this chapter, we're going to cover the following topics:

- Linux Mint distribution
- Linux Mint open source project
- Why Linux Mint is different
- Different Linux Mint editions

Overview

What is Linux Mint? The short answer is a computer operating system based on Linux kernel and GNU tools and libraries. In order to understand what Linux Mint is, first we need to know different concepts such as Linux, kernel, and GNU. Formally, Linux is not an operating system. It's just a software component working as a bridge between applications and the data processing done by the hardware. Because of this fact, the **kernel** is the core component of an operating system. Usually, the term *Linux* is used to refer to a whole operating system based on the kernel. However, an operating system needs more components to be completed. At this point, we look for a family of operating systems based on Linux kernel, plus a set of tools provided by the GNU open source project.

What are GNU tools? Well, first of all we should learn about the GNU project. Basically, this is an open source project started by Richard Stallman with the goal of building a set of software components and tools to avoid the use of any software that is not free. Although GNU tools are compatible with the UNIX operating system, they are different. In fact, GNU is a recursive acronym that means GNU's Not Unix. Due to the quality and popularity of GNU tools many Unix and Unix-like systems, such as GNU/Linux distros, have adopted these tools as components of the whole operating system. The GNU project has some very popular tools such as `bash`, `Emacs`, `gzip`, `automake`, `gcc`, and `make`.

Despite the fact that "Linux" is an accepted term to refer to this family of operating systems, some people and organizations, such as Free Software Foundation, prefer the name GNU/Linux. Keeping this concept in mind, we're going to use GNU/Linux in this book while talking about the whole operating system, and just Linux while referring to the kernel.

Now that we've learned about Linux kernel, and GNU, we can define Linux Mint as a Linux distribution that includes a Linux kernel plus GNU tools and other useful software. Hold on. We've just mentioned a new concept—**distribution**. You almost certianly will have heard of Ubuntu, Fedora, or Debian. These three are examples of Linux distributions, or **distros**. A Linux distribution can be defined as a whole operating system providing a kernel, a system of base tools, and a complete set of applications ready to use.

A bit of history

Clement Lefebvre is a French developer who decided to build a new Linux distro in 2006. His first goal was to experiment and find out if it was possible to apply some design and usability improvements using an existing Linux distro as a base. Before making this decision, Clement spent some time writing articles about other Linux distributions.

Thinking about what could be improved, Clement started to experiment building his own distro. Ubuntu was chosen as the starting point, and after some work, the first Linux Mint version was released in 2006 using **Ada** as the code name. This version was never released as stable. However, a few months later, a new release was ready. Barbara was the chosen name for the Version 2.0 of Linux Mint, which caught the attention and interest of many developers and users. Their feedback was a motivation to continue working on the new operating system. Linux Mint was starting to become one of the most popular operating systems in the world.

Open source project

Linux Mint is not just a Linux distribution; it's an open source project supported by hundreds of volunteers and contributors. This means that people work together sharing ideas, writing tutorials, discussing in forums, and developing software. The final result is not only the Linux distro; a lot of documentation is generated as well. Collective intelligence allows us to build one of the most used operating systems in the world. Remember that the Linux Mint operating system is open source, and it's released under the popular **General Public License GPL** (**GNU**) software license.

Everyone who contributes to the Mint project makes up the **community**. In the open source world, a community is a set of users and developers supporting a specific project. The community of Linux Mint grew very quickly to become an important and essential part of the project.

The community uses a specific website that can be found at `http://community.linuxmint.com`.

Contributing to the project

Everyone can contribute to the Mint project in different ways—that's the magic of open source projects, where the job of each person matters. Usually, people wonder how to contribute to open source projects. Sometimes it's hard to find this kind of information, especially for non-technical people. The Linux Mint website provides enough information about how to contribute to the project. Basically, you can find three different areas of contribution—project contributors, promotion, and financial help. The first area is for those who want to develop software, write documentation, make artwork, or report bugs. However, non-technical people can contribute to this area as well, for instance, they can make translations to get more and more languages supported. The promotion of the project and distro can be for those who are interested in helping others, writing articles, or organizing local presentation for spreading the philosophy and the knowledge of the project. Finally, the financial help is important because the Linux Mint project needs to pay some costs such as hosting or swag stuff.

For more details about how to contribute to the Linux Mint project, please visit `http://www.linuxmint.com/getinvolved.php`.

Why Linux Mint is different

Basically, there are three features that make Mint different. The most important is the user experience. Mint has been designed to provide a very user-friendly desktop with an elegant and sophisticated look and feel. The main menu gives access to applications organized by groups, and the user can launch programs with just a click. Mint developers have created specific tools, integrated with the operating system, to improve the user experience. Some of them include `mintInstall`, `mintUpdate`, `mintBackup`, and `mintUpload`. We'll talk about these software tools later in different chapters of this book. The impatient user can take a look at the GitHub account used by Mint developers at `https://github.com/linuxmint`.

The community behind Linux Mint project is another aspect that makes Mint different than other distros. The organizations and the way they work make Mint different. The feedback provided by users is one of the most valuable resources to improve Mint and to build a better operating system. Other distros have a commercial motivation or developers taking decisions without caring about users' requirements, advices, or ideas.

Finally, Mint includes a lot of software ready to be used out of the box. Multimedia codecs, Java runtime, and Flash Player are installed by default. These features are very important for novice users who need time to get familiarized with the operating system.

Editions

As with other operating systems, Linux Mint has different editions. There are essentially two main editions—one based on Debian, which is called **Linux Mint Debian Edition** (**LMDE**), and another one based on Ubuntu. In addition to Ubuntu and Debian software repositories, Linux Mint uses its specific ones.

LMDE is a rolling release. This means the distro constantly receives updates without generating releases. So it doesn't need to be upgraded. However, releases for the regular Mint edition (the one based on Ubuntu) are only generated by following a specific period of time, this period being longer than the one used for rolling release. Despite LMDE being faster and more responsive than Linux Mint, non-advanced users should think again before using it because continuous updates can bring some errors that they might find difficult to solve. On the other hand, Linux Mint is easy to maintain and was designed to offer an unbeatable user experience.

The Linux Mint project distributes each edition through different ISO images, which can be burned onto a DVD. For LMDE, we can use four images depending on the desktop environment included and the architecture of the processor (32b and 64b).

Regarding the regular edition of Linux Mint, we have more options for choosing so we need to consider that. Specifically, we can use 10 different ISO images. Well, we only have five that are really different, because each has equivalents in both 32b and 64b. Four different desktop environments are included—MATE, Cinnamon, KDE, and Xfce.

Summary

This chapter was a hands-on introduction to the Linux Mint project and distro. We have learned the basic concepts of the Linux Mint operating system and project, including how to contribute to the project and discovering which editions are available.

Now that you are familiar with the main data and information regarding the Linux Mint distro and project, you are ready to install the distro in your own computer.

References

- Linux Mint website: `http://linuxmint.com/`
- The GNU project: `http://www.gnu.org/`
- The GPL license: `http://www.gnu.org/licenses/gpl.html`
- The Linux kernel website: `http://www.kernel.org/`
- Linux Mint download web page: `http://www.linuxmint.com/download.php`

2
Installing Linux Mint

Now that we have looked at the theoretical fundamentals of the Linux Mint project and operating system, it's time to start something practical. Before starting to use an operating system on our computer, we need to install it. This affirmation is not exactly true; some Linux distributions offer a live edition, which allows you to test the operating system without installation. Mint is not an exception and developers distribute ISO live images. Also, the operating system can be installed through the mentioned live images. So, we'll use one of them as an example. In practice, we'll discover how to install Linux Mint on our computer.

In this chapter we shall cover the following topics:

- Creating a bootable USB flash drive for Linux Mint
- Downloading a Linux Mint MATE 13 ISO image
- Booting Linux Mint from an USB drive
- Installing Linux Mint in a computer
- Logging in to the system

Creating a bootable Linux Mint USB flash drive

We're going to install Linux Mint from an ISO image. So, we'll need an external media for burning that image before starting the installation process itself. In *Chapter 1, Introduction to Linux Mint*, we talked about different Linux Mint flavors or editions. Users can choose their own edition based on experience, desktop, and computer architecture. For simplicity we chose MATE edition for 32-bit, and we'll use that edition for learning how to install the operating system. However, the process for creating a bootable flash drive and installing Linux Mint is very similar to other editions.

Make sure you have a USB flash drive ready to use; you'll need one with 2 GB of capacity at least. Although you can find different ways for creating bootable USB devices, we'll work with a program named **Universal Network Installer** (**UNetbootin**). It's an open source program, and you'll find versions for Mac OS X, Windows, and GNU/Linux. The process is identical for those three operating systems, so you can choose your favorite one.

Time for action – downloading and burning the ISO image

For creating our bootable device we'll need to carry out two main tasks—download the ISO image, and burn it using a USB flash drive:

1. Open a web browser and enter the URL `http://mirror.umd.edu/linuxmint/images/stable/13/linuxmint-13-mate-dvd-32bit.iso`.
2. Save the ISO image (`linuxmint-13-mate-dvd-32b.iso`) into your hard drive.
3. Open a new tab or page into your web browser, and enter the URL `http://unetbootin.sourceforge.net.`
4. Click on the button for your operating system.
5. Save the program into your hard drive then install and launch it.
6. When you launch `UNetbootin`, click on the **Diskimage** option and select the downloaded ISO image using the button with the **...** label.

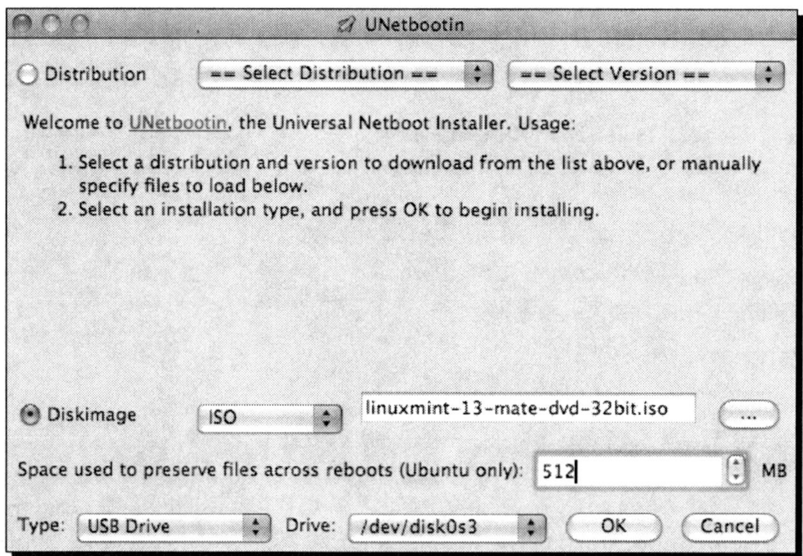

7. Enter a number greater than `256` into the **Space used to preserve file across reboots (Ubuntu only):** input box. We selected **512**, which is enough for our purposes.

8. Select the **USB Drive** option for **Type**, choose your drive unit, and click on the **OK** button. The process will start taking actions such as extracting and copying files, and installing the boot loader. When that process finishes, your flash drive will be ready to use.

What just happened?

As you have discovered, `UNetbootin` is a very simple and useful tool for creating a bootable USB drive from an ISO image. Also, it can be used for downloading a specific GNU/Linux ISO image from the Internet. Actually, the image can be created directly through this option without choosing the ISO file from the system file. Debian, Ubuntu, Gentoo, Fedora, and Mint, among others, are GNU/Linux distributions supported by `UNetbootin`. However, the last version of this software doesn't allow us to download Mint editions greater than 10. So, we chose to download a specific version from one of the official mirrors of Linux Mint, from a web browser.

It's important to fill the input box for the **Space used to preserve file across reboots (Ubuntu only):** option, because Linux Mint is a Ubuntu derived distribution. The amount of chosen MB depends on the space available on your USB drive. This space is reserved for storing some persistent data, such as configuration changes, saved pictures, or databases. Thanks to this kind of storage, you can boot and use a live operating system without installing it.

Keep in mind that the process for creating the bootable USB drive is practically identical on Mac OS X, the Windows family, and GNU/Linux distros.

Installing Linux Mint from a flash drive

Now that we have our bootable USB drive, we're ready for booting and installing Linux Mint. Our downloaded edition is live. This means you can test and use the operating system in your computer without installation. This is a very interesting feature for those who want to try Mint easily. However, we're going to learn how to install Linux Mint on a computer. Before proceeding, make sure your computer has at least 5.7 GB of hard drive space available.

Time for action – booting and installing Linux Mint

Before starting, make sure you have your USB Mint bootable drive ready:

1. Plug your USB drive in your computer.
2. Reboot your computer and select your USB as the device for booting.
3. After booting, you'll see a message indicating that the system will boot automatically in 10 seconds. Before that happens, press the *Enter* key.

4. When the booting splash window appears, leave the default option selected and press *Enter*.
5. After finishing the booting process for Linux Mint, you can see the desktop with a few icons. At this point, Linux Mint live is ready to use but we continue to click on the **Install Linux Mint** icon.

6. Select your language for installation on the **Welcome** dialog box, and click on the **Continue** button.
7. Now, a new window appears and it informs us about the amount of hard drive that is required. Click on the **Continue** button.
8. Linux Mint can be installed on the same computer with other operating systems. You can select the default option or your own partition schema. For simplicity, we'll erase the main hard drive and choose the default option.
9. In the next dialog box, **Erase disk and install Linux Mint**, select the default hard drive, and the installation software will ask you about starting to format the hard drive.
10. Click on the **Install Now** button and a new dialog box will be displayed for choosing your time zone. Click on the **Continue** button when you're ready.
11. Select your keyboard layout, and click on the **Continue** button.
12. Select your username, password, and a name for your computer, then click on **Continue**:

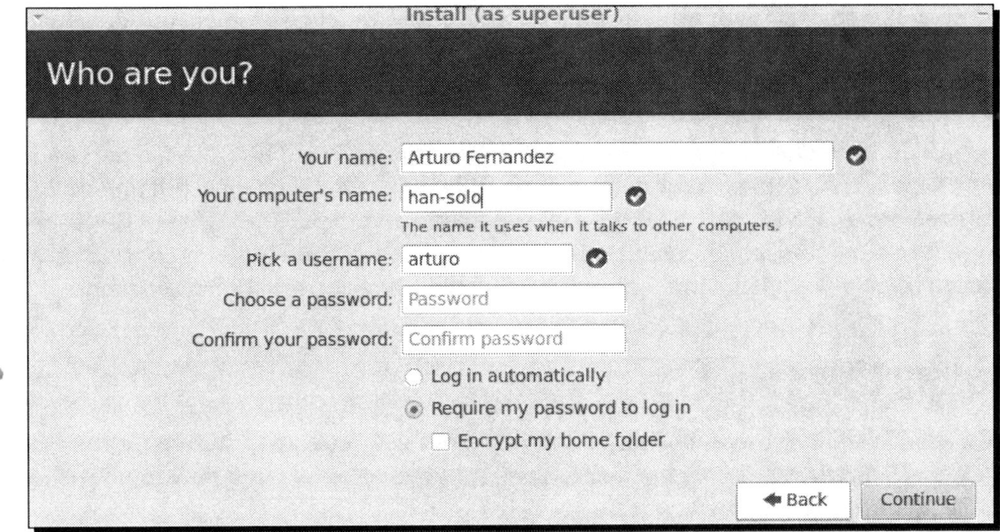

13. Now, Linux Mint will install the required files on your computer. A dialog box will inform you when this process is completed. Finally, remove your USB drive and click on the **Restart Now** button.

What just happened?

Linux Mint offers a comprehensive and easy-to-use wizard for installing the operating system in a computer. A lot of tasks are executed behind the scenes, and they are transparent to the user.

Although the wizard asks you for some information to configure the system, Mint copies the files to the hard drive, detects hardware, configures `bootloader`, and installs all the required software. The process is simple and straightforward, so users don't require any experience with Linux distributions to install Linux Mint.

However, the most complicated step is when you try to install Linux Mint on a computer with different operating systems. Despite that, the wizard will take decisions for you; it could be Useful to make sure what you are doing before proceeding to format your hard drive. Also, it's possible to select a custom partition schema for your hard drive, which is very useful for advanced users. If you are not sure about this kind of data, it's better to leave such decisions to Linux Mint's installation wizard. In that case, you can select the default options.

Usually, Linux Mint will detect all your hardware, but sometimes computers use modern hardware non-compatible with Linux. Some users will find problems because of this and solving them requires advanced knowledge about Linux kernel. However, in most cases, Linux Mint will detect and configure your hardware properly.

If you are going to work with sensible data or you simply prefer to protect your personal data from other users, you can choose to encrypt your home folder. Linux distributions use a specific folder inside the `/home` directory to store data for each user of the operating system. Each user is called through the username; so for username `joe`, the `home` folder will be `/home/joe`. All personal information and custom configuration will be stored in that folder, so it could be worthwhile to encrypt it. Remember that you have chosen a username during the installation process, and Linux Mint has created that user for you. The name of this user will be used for your home folder. Nevertheless, encrypting your `home` folder is considered as an advanced feature, and that's the reason we didn't mark the corresponding checkbox.

Booting Linux Mint

Once the installation process finishes, it's time to boot your operating system for the first time. You will not have to configure anything else, but you should learn how to boot and log in to the system before learning more about Linux Mint.

Time for action – booting Linux Mint for the first time

Booting and logging in to Linux Mint is pretty easy as you'll discover in the following steps:

1. Boot your computer with Linux Mint installed. Make sure any CD, DVD, or USB drives are not connected.
2. Don't pulse any key; Mint will boot automatically.
3. After booting Linux Mint, a new dialog for logging in to the system will be displayed. You should enter your username and password chosen during the installation process:

4. Once your username and password are entered and accepted, Linux Mint will log you in to the system, and you can start using it!

What just happened?

The boot process is always the same and you must get authenticated before starting to use Linux Mint on your computer, unless you choose **Log in automatically** during the installation process. If you change your mind about this feature, don't worry; you can select a different option after the operating system is installed.

To make things easier, Mint developers include an automatic process for booting. It doesn't display any menu or buttons, but it's good to know that the menu exists, and you can select different options to execute other actions, such as launching a memory test or booting in a special mode called **recovery**.

Summary

In this chapter you have learned how to create a bootable Linux Mint USB drive, and how to install and boot the operating system.

Specifically, we covered:

- How to create a bootable USB drive from a downloaded Linux Mint ISO image
- How to install `Linux Mint MATE 32-bit` edition and how to boot it
- How to log in to the system

Now you're ready to use Linux Mint and discover its main features. In the next chapter we'll focus on one of the most important aspects of a Linux distribution—the shell.

3
Basic Shell

In the previous chapter, we learned how to install Linux Mint. Once our operating system is installed on a computer, we're ready to work with it. First, you need to learn about what a shell is, this being one of the most important concepts of the Unix and GNU/Linux operating systems. Then, you'll learn about some interesting and basic usage of the shell, including some useful commands for executing applications, listing files, and finding files inside the file system. Also, we'll go through the fundamental concepts of shell programming.

The following topics will be discussed in the chapter:

- Shell fundamental concepts
- Finding the current directory
- How to run commands and applications
- Finding the absolute path for shell commands
- How to list, examine, and find files
- Redirection and pipelines
- How to set environment variables
- Finding previously executed commands
- Creating a simple shell script
- How to get help

Let's start by learning what a shell is.

What's a shell?

A shell is one of the most important components of a Unix and GNU/Linux operating system. Basically, a shell is software that provides an interface for users, allowing communication with the kernel of an operating system. Using the shell, users can enter commands and execute programs. From a technical point of view, a shell is just a program that can execute other programs on behalf of the user. Usually, a shell is known as a command-line interface, also called **CLI**.

The first Unix operating systems separated the shell from the rest of the components of the operating system. This meant that the shell was a program that could be launched directly by a user. However, other components, such as memory manager, scheduler, and the input/output system worked directly through the kernel without user interaction.

The sixth edition of Unix included a shell as the standard command interpreter. Its name was **sh** and it was developed by Ken Thompson, who worked at Bell Labs. Some time later, in 1979, when the seventh edition of Unix was released, the previous shell (sh) was replaced by a new shell called **Bourne shell**, which was developed by Stephen Bourne. A couple of years later, Bill Joy wrote a new shell and named it **C shell**, also known as **csh**. Joy worked at the University of California and his shell became part of a specific Unix operating system called **Berkeley System Distribution** (**BSD**).

In the mid-1980s, the **Korn shell** (**ksh**) was developed by David Korn, who was then working at the popular AT&T Bell Laboratories. Despite ksh being compatible with the Bourne shell, it includes some additional features that are very useful for programmers and for those who want to apply advanced customizations.

Most of the GNU/Linux distributions include a different shell written as part of the GNU project; its name is **Bourne-Again shell** but it's popularly known as a **Bash shell**. The GNU project developers built Bash with the purpose of getting a shell compatible with the Bourne shell, which would be useful for users and programmers alike.

Therefore, Bash provides a superset of the Bourne functionality. Due to the current popularity of Bash, we're going to learn more about it here. Also, Linux Mint is no exception and it includes Bash as its default shell.

A Bash shell includes commands that you can enter directly. These commands help you to execute useful and common operations, such as changing the current directory, displaying content of a file, or listing the content of a specific directory. Some of these commands are built into the Bash shell itself; others are separate programs included by the GNU/Linux distributions. Both kinds of commands are considered Bash commands, and you'll learn some of them in this chapter.

When you open a shell, you can see some symbols, some text, and a cursor blinking; together these are known as the prompt, which indicates that the shell is ready and you can start entering your commands. The type of information that prompt displays depends on how the prompt was configured. Basically, you'll find data about your username, machine name, and current directory. Usually, the dollar symbol (`$`) acts as a separator between that data and the cursor, which is blinking at the place where you can type.

Where are you?

We're going to start working with the shell and learn how to find out where the current directory is and how to change from one directory to another. Also, we'll discover which application provides a command-line interface for Linux Mint.

Time for action – learning pwd and cd commands

The command-line interface used by Linux Mint is provided by an application called **MATE Terminal**. We'll search it, launch it, and then we're going to learn and execute `pwd` and `cd` commands by following these steps:

1. Click on the **Menu** option located at the bottom of your desktop.
2. After clicking, a new window menu is displayed with a lot of options. On the right-hand side pane, you'll see an area called **Favorites**; there, click on the **Terminal** icon for launching MATE Terminal, as shown in the following screenshot:

3. Now that you have a shell running through MATE Terminal, you're ready to type and launch commands. Our first command will be `pwd`, which returns the path of the current directory. Enter `pwd` directly on the MATE Terminal window.

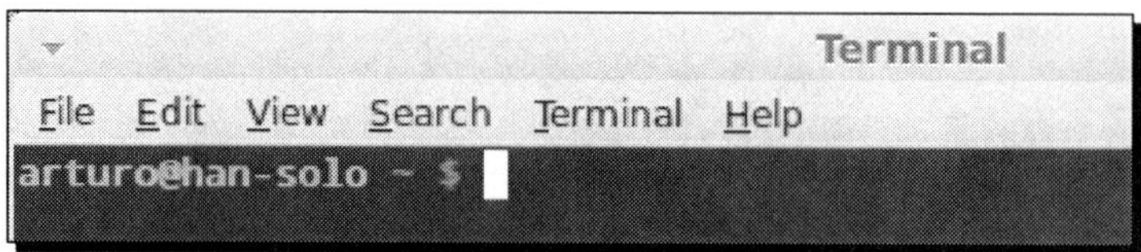

4. When you launch MATE Terminal, your current directory will be your home directory; so the output of the **pwd** command will be that directory, which is evident from the following screenshot:

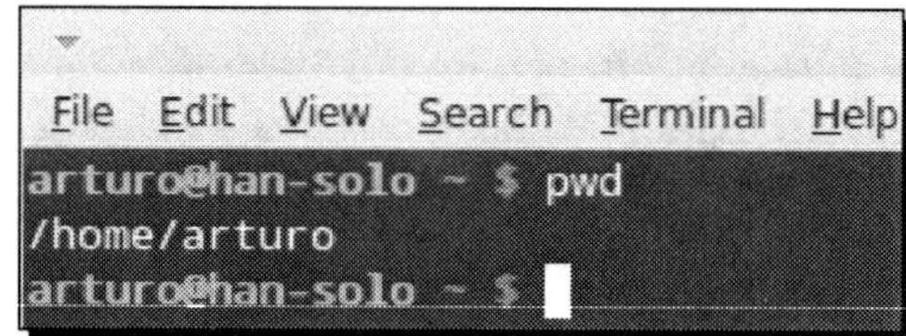

5. We're going to change the current directory, and set `/tmp` as the new current directory by using this command: `arturo@han-solo ~ $ cd /tmp`.
6. After executing the command, we'll discover that the prompt has changed to indicate to us that our current directory is now `/tmp`, as can be seen by looking at `arturo@han-solo /tmp $`.

What just happened?

Because we're working with the MATE edition of Linux Mint, our default command-line interface is provided by MATE Terminal. However, other editions also include similar programs. For example, Cinnamon provides GNOME Terminal as its default CLI application.

MATE Terminal gives us access to the shell, and we can launch commands and programs through it. In fact, MATE Terminal provides a text-based command-line interface using a window with a graphical user interface. We've learned our first command for displaying what is our current directory. This action is important, because the output of some other commands depends on that directory.

The `cd` command is useful for changing the current directory and setting some other directory as the new current directory inside the filesystem. The first argument that is passed for the `cd` command is the path of the directory that you want to set as the new current directory.

It's important to know that the ~ symbol indentifies your home directory, so you can use it as a shortcut instead of typing the full path.

Keep in mind that your prompt will look different because your username and machine name will be different from mine. In our examples, the username is `arturo`, and the machine name is `han-solo`. Yes, you guessed it, I'm a Star Wars fan!

Have a go hero – using a shortcut for accessing your home directory

Try to execute the `cd` command without arguments and you'll discover how the current directory changes to your home directory. The following is a shortcut to change to that directory quickly:

```
arturo@han-solo /tmp $ cd
arturo@han-solo ~ $
```

MATE Terminal can be configured and customized in different ways. For example, you can change the font type and size and set a specific color scheme. You can take a look at the **Profile preferences** menu from the **Edit** option.

Running commands

As you have learned, the shell allows us to communicate directly with the operating system of your computer. This action helps us launch commands and applications. Previously, you discovered how to launch commands such as `cd` and `pwd` by just entering each command and then pressing *Enter*. However, some commands are used to invoke programs using a full path. Now you'll learn how to do that.

Time for action – launching a program from the command line

Assume that a program called `testme exists`, which can be found inside the `/tmp` directory. We can invoke this program by following these steps:

1. Open a shell using the MATE Terminal application.
2. Type `/tmp/testme` and hit *Enter*.
3. The output of the program will be displayed on the shell. If the invoked program has a graphical user interface, a new window will be opened.

What just happened?

When you enter a command, it is executed directly, because there exists an environment variable to find all the files that can be executed. The name of that variable is `$PATH`, and its value indicates where the shell should look for executable files. Commands and applications are executables files, but not all of them are located in the directories associated to `$PATH`. That's the reason for using the complete path for invoking any file. Following this rule, we invoked the `testme` file through its pathname.

How does the operating system know which files are executable? It's easy—executable files use a specific flag that indicates this property to the operating system; the shell knows this and can execute them easily.

If your current directory is where an executable file is located, you can invoke it using a dot plus a slash (`./`), followed by the name of the file. Thanks to this technique, you don't need to use the full path or modify the `$PATH` variable. For example, our example `testme` command can be invoked by using the following commands:

```
arturo@han-solo ~ $ cd /tmp
arturo@han-solo /tmp $ ./testme
```

Some commands and programs allow us to pass additional parameters; each one must be preceded by a blank space. We'll learn about these kinds of commands (at least some commands) later.

Have a go hero – executing programs without using the full path

You can try and modify `$PATH` for adding the `/tmp` directory, and then you can directly call the `testme` command without using its full path. For more information about how to set environment variables, see the *Setting environment variables* section later in this chapter.

Search commands

Sometimes it is important to search for the full path of a command or an executable file, which can be located through the `$PATH` variable. The most useful command for taking that action is `which`, so now we'll explain how to use it.

Time for action – using the which command

Before proceeding, make sure you have launched MATE Terminal. Then perform these steps:

1. Enter the following command:

   ```
   arturo@han-solo ~ $ which find
   ```

2. The `which` command will display the following output:

```
/usr/bin/find
```

What just happened?

The `which` shell command is included in most of the GNU/Linux distributions, even in Linux Mint. Thanks to that command, we can get the full path of a command or an executable file, which can be located through the `$PATH` variable. On the other hand, the `find` command is a program for finding files; you'll learn more about it in this chapter.

Listing, examining, and finding files

A file is a persistent resource for storing information. Images, sounds, programs, and commands use files that can be managed by users. Due to that fact, it's important to learn how to list, examine, and find files through our shell.

Time for action – using the ls, locate, find, and cat commands

We're going to use a few commands such as `find`, `locate`, `cat`, and `ls`. The last one is used for displaying the content of a directory, whereas the `find` and `locate` commands are used for finding files in our filesystem. The `cat` command is used for getting the content of a file as output. Don't forget to make sure that your shell is running.

1. First, we'll execute `ls` directly from our home directory; we only need to enter `ls` in our command-line interface.
2. The output for the previous command will be something like the following:

```
Desktop  Documents  Downloads  Music  Pictures  Public  Templates
Videos
```

3. Now, we'll continue looking for all those files with a `.conf` extension (`*.conf`) inside the `/etc/ufw` directory by using the following command:

```
arturo@han-solo ~ $ find /etc/ufw -name '*.conf'
```

4. As an output of the `find` command, you'll find all files with a `.conf` extension inside your home directory:

```
/etc/ufw/sysctl.conf
/etc/ufw/ufw.conf
```

5. The `locate` command is used when we know the name of the file that we're trying to find. Imagine you want to look for the `.bash_history` file but you don't remember the directory where the file resides; in this case, you can use the following command:

   ```
   arturo@han-solo ~ $ locate .bash_history
   ```

6. The result of the command last executed will be as follows:

   ```
   /home/arturo/.bash_history
   ```

7. Finally, we'll use the `cat` command for displaying the content of a text file. Let's list the content of the filesystem that contains information related to your network interfaces, by using the following command:

   ```
   arturo@han-solo ~ $ cat /etc/network/interfaces
   ```

8. As a result, you'll get the contents of the `/etc/network/interfaces` file displayed as follows:

   ```
   auto lo
   iface lo inet loopback
   ```

What just happened?

The `find` and `locate` commands are very useful when you need to find a file or a group of files. Different parameters can be used for each command, and we have learned the basic use of each of them. It's important to know that the `find` command starts searching from the current directory. However, `locate` searches using a specific database without bothering about the current directory. This means `locate` can find files that aren't inside the current directory. Both commands use a search algorithm that is based on patterns. Remember, we used the `*.conf` pattern as a parameter for the `find` command.

The `ls` command is one of the most used in Linux systems, because it offers basic information about the content of a directory. Quite often, you need that information before taking actions through the shell. This command supports a lot of different parameters that allow you to get different kinds of information about the content of a directory.

As part of printing the contents of a text file, the `cat` command can concatenate the content of different files, thereby displaying all the information directly on the shell. Each file can be passed as an argument to the `cat` command.

Have a go hero – getting more information when listing files

If you want to get more information about each file inside a directory, you can try to launch the `ls` command with `-l` as an argument, as shown here:

```
arturo@han-solo ~ $ ls -l
```

Also, it could be interesting to execute the `find` command by passing a different extension than JPEG as a parameter.

Two more commands can help you to display the content of a text file—`more` and `less`. Both commands allow you to read the content on your screen without the risk of some modification by accident. You only need to pass the name of the text file as an argument to each of these commands.

Pipelines and redirection

In Unix and GNU/Linux operating systems, it is very common to take the output of one command and use it as an input for another command. Because of this concept, it's possible to create a combination of commands using only a single line in the shell. We're going to use a simple example for illustrating the use of pipelines. Specifically, we'll look for a string inside a text file.

Redirection is another powerful and common technique that allows us to append the output of a command to any other file available in our machine's filesystem. To make things easier, we'll just create a text file with the current date.

Time for action – using pipelines and redirection by applying different commands

Let's look at how pipelines work:

1. Enter the following command on your shell:

   ```
   $ cat mytext.txt | grep This
   ```

2. You'll get the following output:

   ```
   This is the content for the mytext.txt file
   ```

3. Now, we're going to use redirection for creating a new file that contains some content:

   ```
   $ date > current_date.txt
   ```

4. Check the new file to make sure the content is valid, by using the following command:

   ```
   $ cat current_date.txt
   Sat Sep 23 14:41:29 CEST 2012
   ```

What just happened?

Although we used simple examples for understanding pipelines and redirection, it's possible to create complicated commands through these techniques. It depends on the ability and experience of the user.

As you must have realized, we used the | character for indicating that we're going to use a pipeline. It's possible to use that character multiple times with different commands.

As far as redirection is concerned, the > character is used to store the output of a command in a file. On the other hand, `date` is a simple application for getting the current date. Finally, the `cat` command helps you to print the content of the new file called `current_date.txt`.

Have a go hero – appending content to a file using redirection

Instead of creating a new file, it's possible to append content to an existing file; you only need to use the >> character. For example, we can add more content to an existing file by using the following command:

```
$ echo 'More text' >> current_date.txt
```

Setting environment variables

An environment variable defines some aspects that can affect the behavior of programs and commands running in an operating system. Each environment variable has a value that can be changed dynamically through the shell. Usually, an operating system creates and sets some environment variables, but users can change these and add new variables. Default applications such as a web browser, text editor, and music player can be defined using environment variables. The shell uses this kind of variable to get information about a user's environment and sets this data to the commands and programs. We'll learn how to get and set a value to a specific environment variable.

Time for action – setting the PATH environment variable

Perform the following steps to set up the `PATH` environment variable:

1. Launch MATE Terminal, and get ready to enter some commands.
2. Enter the following command:
   ```
   $ PATH=$PATH:/tmp
   ```
3. Get the value of the `PATH` variable by using this command:
   ```
   $ echo $PATH
   ```

4. You'll get something like the following:

```
/usr/local/sbin:/usr/local/bin:/usr/sbin:/usr/bin::/sbin/bin:/usr/
games:/tmp
```

What just happened?

The value of an environment variable is set directly into the shell; we only need to use the = character along with a desired value for the variable. In our example, we used the PATH variable and added a new value, the /tmp directory. Obviously, we could have just used a simpler value, but in the case of PATH we want to keep its original value as well.

The echo command accepts as argument any kind of literal and outputs that literal to the standard output. If you want to get the value of an environment variable, you should prefix it by the $ symbol. Therefore, the echo $PATH command will output the value for the PATH environment variable.

Have a go hero – learning the export command

You can get the values of different environment variables, such as HOME, TERM, and EDITOR. Also, you can change their values dynamically.

If you want the value of an environment variable to be available for the shell that is created from an original one, you should use the export command:

```
$ export TERM=/bin/bash
```

Displaying command history

Usually, people working with a shell execute a lot of commands, so it can be very useful to get a history of executed commands. Thanks to the history command, we can find out which commands were executed previously.

Time for action – using the history command

I'm very sure that you've been executing some shell commands, so we're ready to use the history command directly:

1. Enter history in the shell.
2. Based on the command that you entered in the past, you'll get a list similar to the following:

```
cd /tmp
which find
```

What just happened?

Each command you type on the shell is stored in a file called `.bash_history`, which is read by the `history` command for showing you the information about previously executed commands. The operating system stores one `.bash_history` file for each user, and this file resides in the home directory of the user.

Have a go hero – checking the history of executed commands

If you're looking for a command that you executed previously, you can combine the `history` and `grep` commands along with pipelines for getting this information. Imagine you want to know which `cd` commands were executed previously; in this case you can type the following command:

```
$ history | grep cd
```

Also, left and right cursors provide you navigation over the last executed commands.

Creating your first shell script

So far, we have launched commands by directly typing into the shell and pressing *Enter*, but it's also possible to use a text file for writing a set of commands and launch this file through the shell. This technique allows us to create scripts or small applications for launching commands or executing different shell operations. In fact, the Bash shell offers us a particular domain-specific programming language for this purpose. Although the learning curve for this specific programming language is not trivial, we're going to learn how to create a simple Bash script for executing some commands using control structures.

In our example, we'll create a script for checking whether a text file exists. If the answer is in the affirmative, we'll launch a message informing you about it. Otherwise, we'll create a new text file with a single line. Finally, whatever happens, we'll list the created text file.

Time for action – creating and executing a shell script

We need to use a text editor; of course, you can use your favorite one. Linux Mint offers us several text editors such as Vim, Emacs, and Pluma. The latter has a graphical user interface and is installed by default, so we'll use it for our work. Here's how to get started:

1. Click on the **Menu** button, and then click on the **Text Editor** menu option, as shown in the following screenshot:

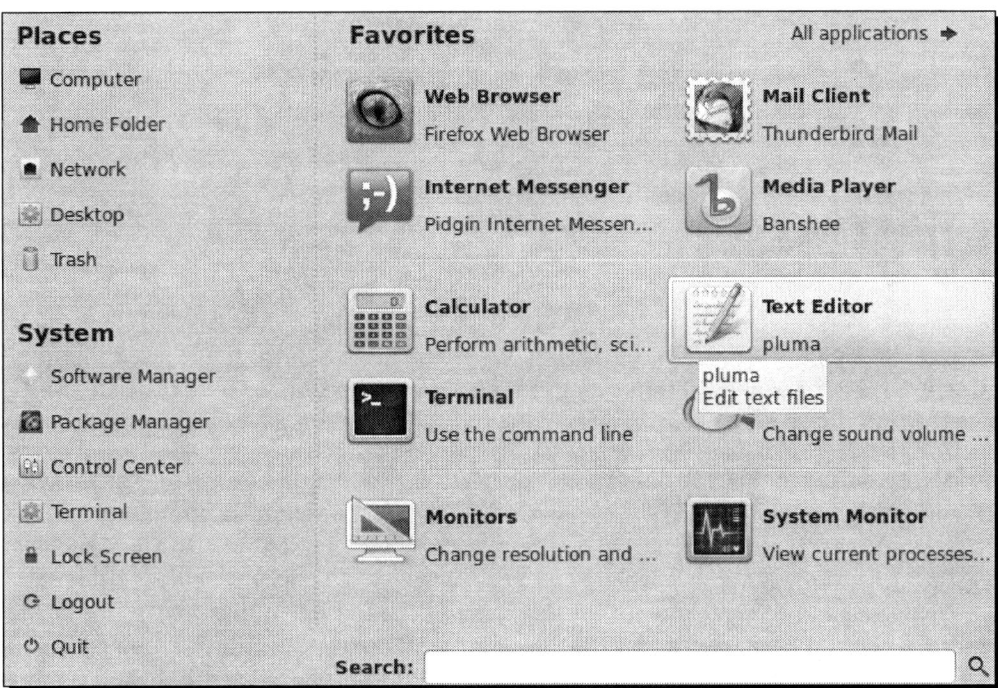

2. A new window will be displayed, and you'll be ready to use Pluma. Enter the following lines, and save the file as `myscript.sh` when you're ready:

```
#!/bin/bash
if [ -f "myfile.txt" ]
then
    echo "Sorry, file already exists."
else
    echo "Content for file" > myfile.txt
fi
ls -l myfile.txt
```

3. Give execution permissions to your new shell script:

```
$ chmod +x myscript.txt
```

4. Launch your script:

```
$ ./myscript.sh
```

5. The output of the last command should be something like the following:

```
-rw-rw-r--. 1 arturo arturo 17 Oct 20 11:12 myfile.txt
```

6. Also, you can check the content of the created file by using the `cat` command:

```
$ cat myfile.txt
```

What just happened?

All shell scripts are plain text files, so you can use any text editor for writing this kind of program. The first line of a shell script should start by indicating which kind of shell will be used for executing the script. The default shell in Linux Mint is Bash, so we'll use that for our shell scripts. This is the reason for using the `/bin/bash` executable file in the first line of our shell script. As you have may realized, two special symbols have been used in that line.

The first one indicates that the line is a comment, and the second one is used for knowing what kind of shell should execute the shell script. The `if` statement is conditional and it checks if a certain condition is met. In our case, it checks if `myfile.txt` exists. If the answer is negative, the `else` statement will be executed, where we'll create a new file using the `echo` command and redirect the output to it. Finally, the last line of the shell script will be executed without it bothering about the conditional statement. To test this, you can launch the command twice; you will find that the output is different, because the second time the file will exist, as it was created before.

In the third step, we used a command called `chmod`, which is very useful for changing permissions for a file. We'll learn more about this command in the next chapter, but in our shell script we only add an execution permission for it. Once we have this kind of permission for our shell script, we can invoke it directly through the command line.

Have a go hero – learning advanced shell programming

Although our example is very simple, you can learn more about shell programming from the following resources:

- *Bash Programming – Introduction How-To*, from `http://bit.ly/x24V3`
- *Advanced Bash-Scripting Guide*, from `http://tldp.org/LDP/abs/html/`
- *Debian Bash Programming Guide*, from `http://bit.ly/Qs12TQ`

How to get help

Getting help about shell commands and some executables files is easy thanks to two commands, `man` and `info`. Both of them are included in Linux Mint; let's discover how to use them.

Time for action – using the man and the info commands

Follow these steps to better understand how the `man` and the `info` commands can be used:

1. Again, make sure your shell is running.
2. Execute the following command to get information about the `ls` command:

   `arturo@han-solo ~ $ man ls`

3. The following screenshots show you the output of the previously executed command:

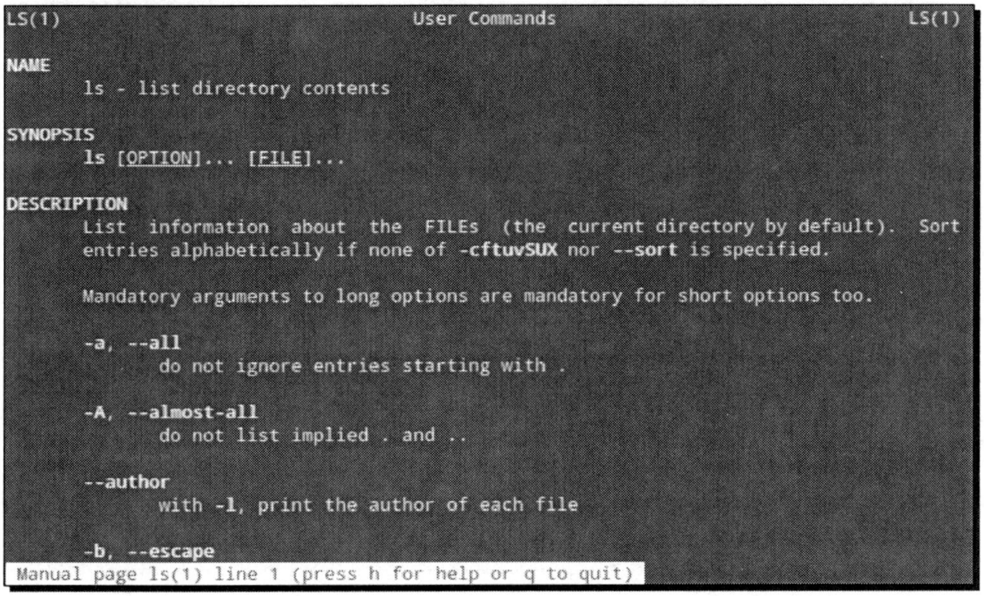

```
LS(1)                          User Commands                          LS(1)

NAME
       ls - list directory contents

SYNOPSIS
       ls [OPTION]... [FILE]...

DESCRIPTION
       List  information  about  the  FILEs  (the  current directory by default).  Sort
       entries alphabetically if none of -cftuvSUX nor --sort is specified.

       Mandatory arguments to long options are mandatory for short options too.

       -a, --all
              do not ignore entries starting with .

       -A, --almost-all
              do not list implied . and ..

       --author
              with -l, print the author of each file

       -b, --escape
 Manual page ls(1) line 1 (press h for help or q to quit)
```

4. Now, it's time to test the `info` command:

   `arturo@han-solo ~ $ info ls`

5. After executing the `info` command, you'll get the following information:

```
File: coreutils.info,  Node: ls invocation,  Next: dir invocation,  Up:

10.1 `ls': List directory contents
==================================

The `ls' program lists information about files (of any type, including
directories).  Options and file arguments can be intermixed
arbitrarily, as usual.

   For non-option command-line arguments that are directories, by
default `ls' lists the contents of directories, not recursively, and
omitting files with names beginning with `.'.  For other non-option
arguments, by default `ls' lists just the file name.  If no non-option
argument is specified, `ls' operates on the current directory, acting
as if it had been invoked with a single argument of `.'.

   By default, the output is sorted alphabetically, according to the
locale settings in effect.(1) If standard output is a terminal, the
output is in columns (sorted vertically) and control characters are
output as question marks; otherwise, the output is listed one per line
and control characters are output as-is.

   Because `ls' is such a fundamental program, it has accumulated many
--zz-Info: (coreutils.info.gz)ls invocation, 57 lines --Top-----------
Welcome to Info version 4.13. Type h for help, m for menu item.
```

What just happened?

The `man` command offers you a lot of information about how the executable or Bash commands work. As a parameter, the `man` command receives the name of the Bash command or executable file for displaying information. This command reads a file or a set of files written in a specific format so developers can include documentation for programs using that format.

Also, the `info` command displays some useful information about commands. However, the documentation format used by `info` is different to that used by `man`. As you must have noticed, even though we used the same argument for both the commands, their outputs were different. Some users prefer `man` and others `info`, but basically both offer similar information.

Summary

We learned a lot in this chapter about the shell and basic commands, including how to create a simple shell script. Specifically, we covered the following:

- Basic usage of the shell through the MATE Terminal application
- Looking for the current directory where your shell is pointing
- Running executable commands and files
- Getting the full path of commands and executable files referred by the `PATH` environment variable
- How to use the `ls` command for listing files
- How to use the `find` and `locate` commands for finding files
- How to display content for a text file through the `cat` command
- Using pipeline and redirection techniques
- Setting the `PATH` environment variable
- How to use the `history` command for finding which commands were executed previously
- Shell programming fundamentals
- How to get help about shell and its commands

Once you know the basic shell concepts and commands, you're ready to learn about one of the most important tasks for system administrators—how to provision user accounts.

4
Account Provisioning

Creating users and groups is one of the most important and basic tasks for system administrators. Before learning more advanced concepts, it's essential to know how to deal with users' accounts and groups.

In this chapter we will cover the following:

- Finding out the current user
- Becoming the root user
- Changing a user's password
- Adding a new user
- Adding a new group
- Adding a user to a specific group
- Changing user privileges

Who am I?

A user account is required for accessing Linux Mint. Actually, when you installed the operating system, you typed some data about a user, and his or her account was created. Sometimes the system administrator needs to become a different user of the system, so it's interesting to know which user is currently using the shell. We're going to explain how to do that.

Time for action – finding out the current user

Before proceeding, you should launch the **MATE Terminal** application.

1. Type the following command in the shell:

```
$ whoami
```

2. As the output of the previously executed command, you'll get the name of the user who is currently using the shell; in our case it will be the following:

```
arturo
```

What just happened?

You have learned how to use the `whoami` command for identifying which user is currently logged in and using the shell. This command is pretty simple, and it just returns the username without additional information.

Becoming the root user

Each GNU/Linux operating system works with a super user called **root**. This is a special user of the operating system that is used by the system administrator. The root user has all kinds of permissions over files and programs. Actually, some specific operations can only be executed through this user.

Linux Mint doesn't enable the root user by default. However, Mint uses special commands that allow users to become the root user. This means that regular users can execute actions that were initially reserved for the root user. Also, Mint configures the `sudo` command, allowing the user created during the installation process to become the root user.

Time for action – using the sudo command to become the root user

We're going to use the `sudo` command to become the root user using the shell:

1. Open the **MATE Terminal** application.
2. Type the following command and press the *Enter* key when you're ready:

```
arturo@han-solo ~ $ sudo su -
```

3. A new prompt message will be displayed, asking you for your password:

```
[sudo] password for arturo:
```

4. Type in your password and press the *Enter* key, and you'll get a new prompt like the following one; the current user is root:

```
@han-solo ~ #
```

What just happened?

The `sudo` command allows you to execute a command as another user. Linux Mint is configured by default to allow the user created during the installation process to become the root user directly. You only need to execute the `sudo` command, passing `su -` as a parameter. The first parameter identifies the root user and the second one indicates that Bash initialization files for `root` should be executed. Keep in mind that the `sudo` command will ask you for the password of the user that is executing that command.

You will have realized that the prompt is different after becoming `root`. The `#` symbol is used for indicating that the current user is `root` instead of the `$` character, which is used for regular users of the system.

Have a go hero – executing the whoami command after becoming the root user

Try to execute the `whoami` command after becoming `root` to check the current user. The output of that command will be `root`.

Changing password

In some cases, system administrators need to change the password of a user. For example, when a user forgets his password, he can the system administrator for a new one.

A password should be provided when a user is created, but each user should change their password when accessing the system for the first time.

The process of changing your own password is not hard; you can do it through a simple application that is installed by default in Linux Mint.

Time for action – changing the password for a user

Each user of the system can change their own password using a GUI application provided by Linux Mint. We're going to learn how to do that now:

1. Click on the **Menu** button and click again on the **All Applications** button located on the right-hand side of the **Favorites** pane.

2. Click on the **Administration** menu option.

3. A set of new options will be displayed, so you only need to click on the **Users and Groups** menu option as shown in the following screenshot:

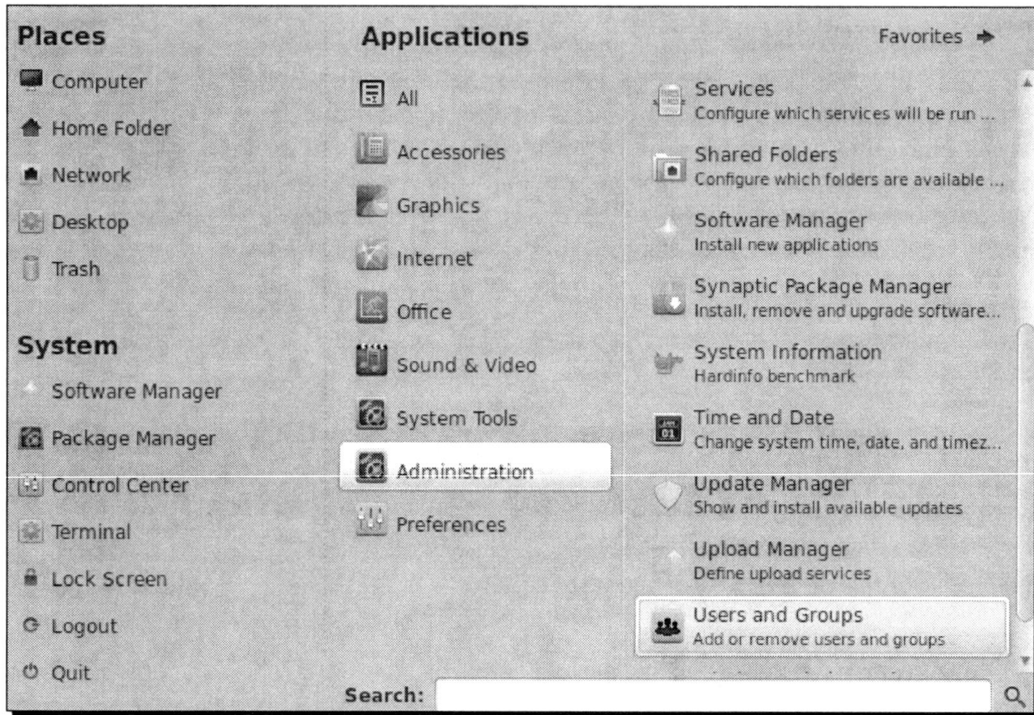

4. After clicking on **Users and Groups**, a dialog box asking for your password will be displayed. Type your password and click on the **Authenticate** button:

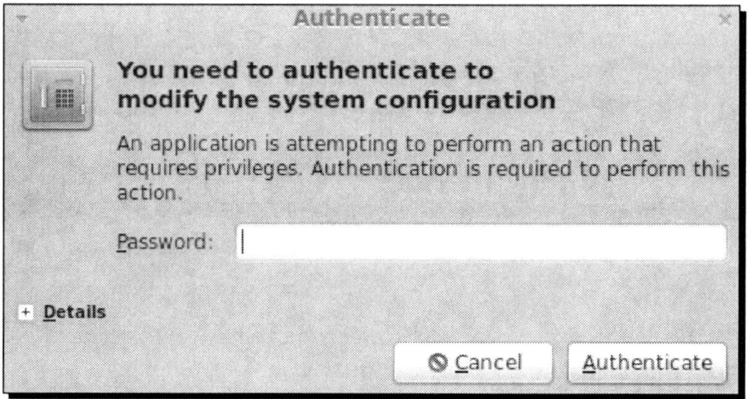

5. A new window will be displayed if your password is correct. This is the Linux Mint application for dealing with users and groups:

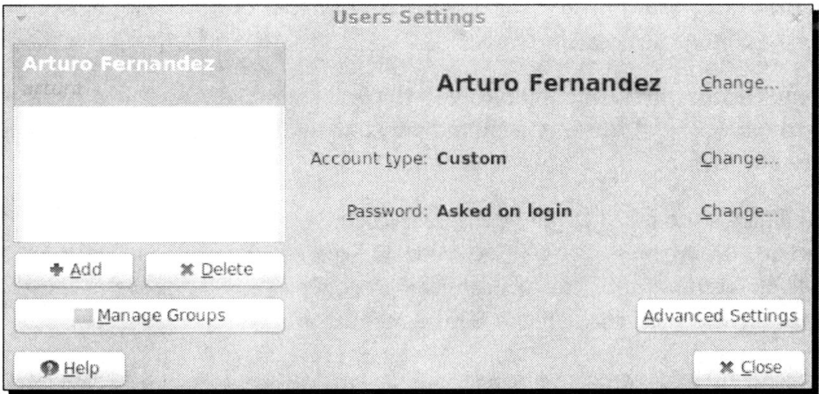

6. Click on the **Change...** button close to the **Password: Asked on login** option.

7. The following window allows you to change your password. First, you should type your current password. Then you can select the **Set password by hand** option and type your new password in the **New password** and **Confirmation** input boxes. When you're ready, click on the **OK** button:

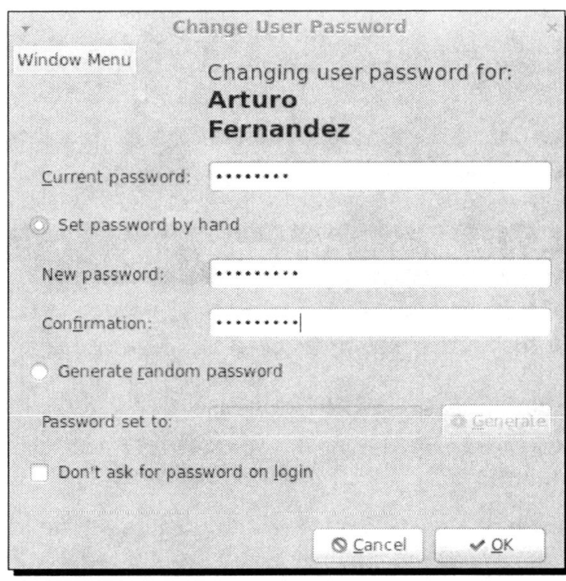

8. Right now, a dialog box asking for your confirmation will be displayed; click on **Yes** and your password will be changed.

What just happened?

Changing your password is pretty simple, thanks to the GUI application provided by Linux Mint. Behind the scenes, Mint calls the `passwd` command for applying your changes, allowing you to change your password.

The **Users and Groups** application allows you to perform more operations related to users and groups. Some of these operations only can be executed by `root`, so you should authenticate this user before proceeding.

In the same dialog used for changing your password, you also can choose whether you want to be logged in with/without using a password. On the other hand, a random password can automatically be generated by the application. You only need to select the **Generate random password** option and then click on the **Generate** button.

Have a go hero – using the passwd command

You can change your password directly at the command line with the `passwd` command. Just type the command and follow the instructions on the screen.

Also, you can change the password for another user. In order to do that, you must become the root user and execute the `passwd` command, passing the username of the user whose password needs to be changed as an argument.

Adding a new user

As system administrator, one of the most common tasks is to create new users for the system. It's an easy task, thanks to the **Users and Groups** application included in Linux Mint.

Time for action – creating a new user

We need to launch the **Users and Groups** application, so make sure this application is running. Our purpose is to create a new user called `Luke`, whose username will be `luke`.

1. Click on the **Add** button located on the left-hand side of the main window.
2. A dialog box will be displayed; type in your password and click on the **Authenticate** button.
3. Right now you can see a new window with two different input boxes, one for the name and another for the username. Type `Luke` for the first one and `luke` for the second one. Click on the **OK** button when you are ready:

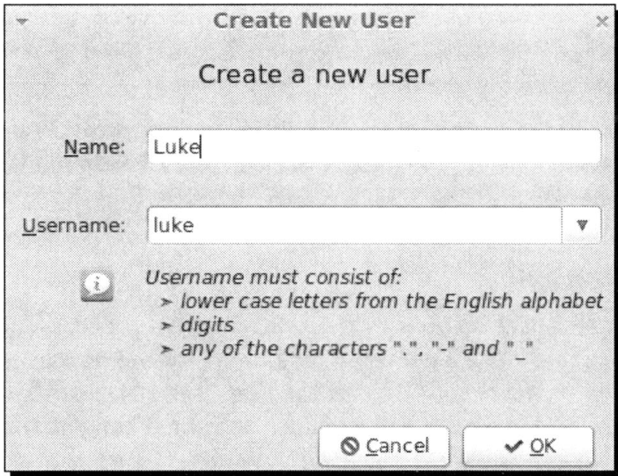

4. A new window will be displayed, asking you to choose a password for the new user. Type a new password or select the **Generate random password** option. Click on the **OK** button to continue.
5. As a result, you will see that the new user is displayed on the user's list of the system:

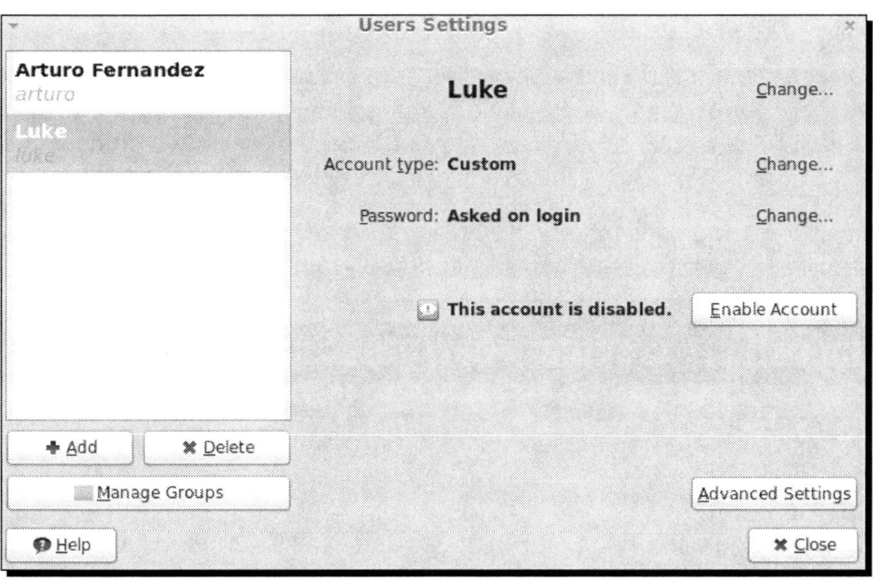

6. If you observe the data of the new user, you'll discover a message informing you that the account for the new user is disabled, so we need to activate it by clicking on the **Enable Account** button.
7. After clicking on the **Enable Account** button, a window for changing the password will be displayed. Change the password again and click on the **OK** button. Now, the account is enabled.

What just happened?

We've just created a new user account by following a simple process. The GUI is pretty intuitive and allows us to choose a name and username for the new user. Each user should have a password, so we need to type one for the new user. For security reasons, new accounts are disabled, and you must activate each account, changing the password.

Have a go hero – try to delete a user

Also, you can delete user accounts through the **Delete** button associated with each listed user of the **Users and Groups** tool. If you click on that button, a new dialog is displayed asking for confirmation to delete the specified user.

Adding a new group

In GNU/Linux systems, users can be categorized into groups. Basically, a **group** is a set of users who share permissions. Groups allow system administrators to work with users in an organized way. For example, a specific group can have access to certain directories. This means that all users belonging to that group can access these specific directories.

Linux Mint uses many groups by default; some of them are **audio**, **backup**, **games**, **irc**, and **lp**. Also, it's possible to create additional custom groups. We'll learn how to do that.

Time for action – creating a new group called develop

We'll continue using the GUI application for managing users and groups, so make sure it's running before continuing. We'll create a new group called `develop`.

1. Click on the **Manage Groups** button.
2. A new window showing all the existing groups will be displayed. Click on the **Add** button to continue.

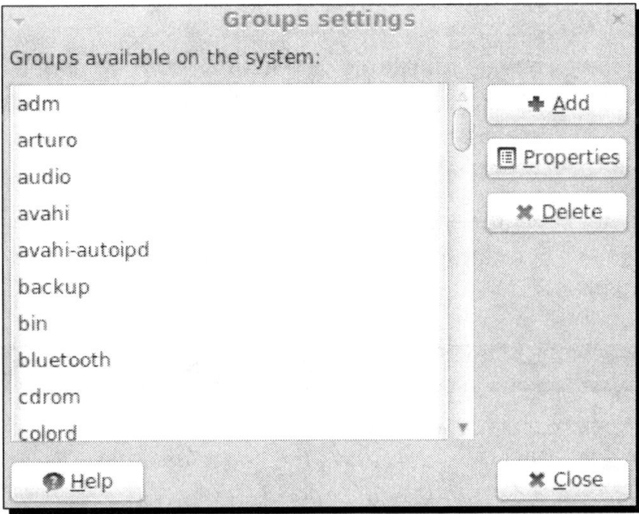

3. Type in your password and click on the **Authenticate** button. Right now you can see a new window called **New group**.
4. Type `develop` in the **Group name** input box and click on the **OK** button, as shown in the following screenshot:

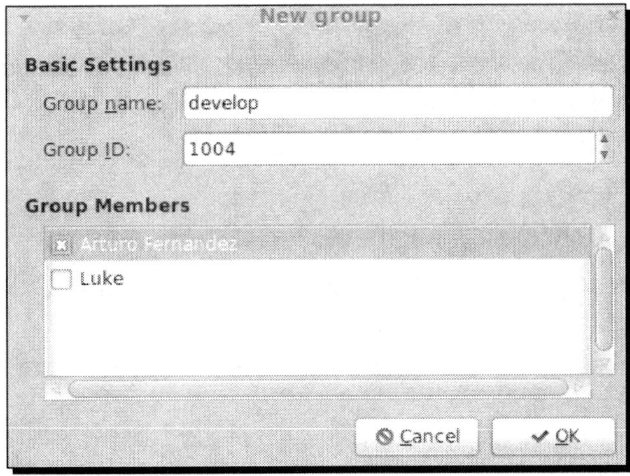

5. As a result, you can see how the newly developed group is displayed in the list of existing groups.

What just happened?

The window for creating a new group allows us to choose a group name and group ID for it. This number identifies each group and must be different for each group created in the system. Linux Mint will choose a group ID by default for every new group, but you can choose a different number as well.

When you're creating a new group, it's also possible to add users to it directly. A list of users will be displayed so you can select some of them, and Mint will add this user to a new group automatically.

Have a go hero – try to delete a group

Deleting a group is pretty easy; you only need to select a group and click on the **Delete** button. Before taking this action, you'll need to confirm the delete operation. Don't forget that you need to click on the **Manage Groups** button to access the list of groups on the system.

Adding a user to a group

If you need to add a user to a group, you can do it easily. You only need to access group properties and choose which users should belong to the specified group.

Time for action – adding the user luke to the develop group

Once more, make sure the **Users and Groups** tool is running. We're going to add the user **luke** to the **develop** group, which was created previously.

1. Click on the **Manage Groups** button.
2. Select the **develop** group and click on the **Properties** button.
3. A new window shows you the properties of the selected group, including a list of users. Select **luke** from the list and click on the **OK** button.
4. Authenticate with your password on the modal window, and click on the **Authenticate** button.
5. The user **luke** has been added to the **develop** group.

What just happened?

While accessing group properties, we have the choice of adding users to a group. You can select one or more users from the list of existing users displayed in the properties window of the selected group.

Changing user privileges

Linux and Unix operating systems use the concept of **user privilege**, which is a right or authorization to execute an action. Therefore, users need **privileges** or **permissions** for either creating or deleting a file, accessing a printer, or executing a command.

The operating system provides a set of users and groups with some permissions over files, directories, and devices. However, system administrators can modify this default configuration. Also, it's possible to assign specific permissions for custom users and groups.

Mint provides a graphic tool for managing user privileges easily. Let's look at how to use it.

Time for action – granting permissions to a user for monitoring system logs

We're going to grant access for monitoring system logs to our user **luke**. This is a simple example to illustrate how to change user privileges. Obviously, you can apply similar steps for changing different permissions:

1. Launch the **Users and Groups** tool.
2. Select the user **luke** from the users list, and click on the **Advanced Settings** button.
3. Type your password when the dialog box asks for it.
4. After clicking on the **OK** button, select the **User Privileges** tab.
5. Now you have a list of privileges that can be granted to or revoked from the user **luke**. Select **Monitor system logs** and click on the **OK** button, as shown in the following screenshot:

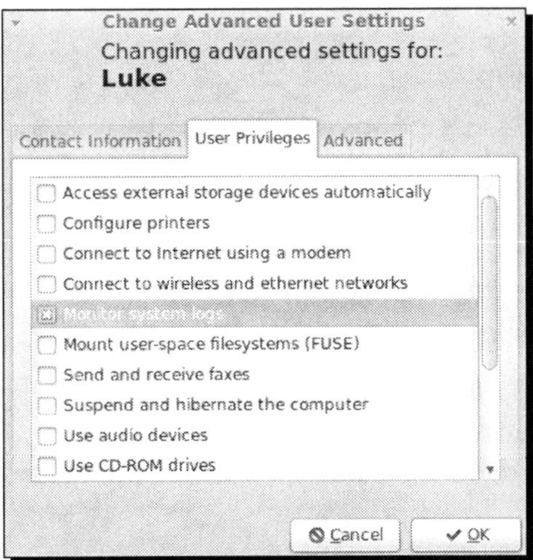

6. At this point, the user **luke** is ready to read the special files used for monitoring the system.

What just happened?

The advanced settings for each user provided by the **User and Groups** tools allow you to manage permissions in a very easy and efficient way. You have a list of privileges that can be applied for each user. Natural language is used, so you don't need to know advanced concepts to assign permissions to users.

Have a go hero – using command line for changing permissions

Although Mint offers you a graphic tool for working with user privileges, you can use the shell for the same purpose. One of the most useful commands is `chmod`, which allows you to change permissions for files and directories. Also, thanks to the `chown` command, you can decide who the owner is of a specific file or directory.

If you're interested in both commands, you should use the `man` and `info` commands to get more information about the `chmod` and `chown` commands.

For permissions and users, Mint provides three predefined account types, namely **Custom**, **Administrator**, and **desktop user**. You can choose one of these for each user; the **Account type** option provides access to this functionality.

Summary

In this chapter you learned the basic operations for account provisioning.

Specifically, we covered the following:

- Discovering the current user
- How to create users and groups
- Adding a user to a group
- Becoming the root user
- Changing the user's password
- Changing user privileges

By this point, you will have understood the basic concepts and ideas about how to work with the shell and how to provision user accounts. Now it's time to learn about something very important in the daily work of a system administrator—how to install and configure software.

5

Installing, Removing, and Upgrading Software

In this chapter, you're going to learn one of the most important and basic tasks done by system administrators. These tasks are related to software, specifically how to install, remove, and keep your operating system up-to-date.

In this chapter we will cover the following:

- Installing software
- Removing installed software
- Applying upgrades

Installing software

Sooner or later, system administrators need to install software in one or more machines. In fact, this is one of the most common tasks for the users of this kind of operating system. Linux Mint includes thousands of software applications that can be installed easily. Remember that when you install the operating system, a lot of software is installed by default. Also, it's possible to install additional software provided by Linux Mint. In order to facilitate the process of installing software in Linux Mint, this operating system includes a tool named **Software Manager**.

Time for action – installing the AbiWord word processor

We're going to install a text processor called **AbiWord** (`http://www.abisource.com`) using the Software Manager application. Let us see how this is done:

1. Click on the **Menu** button and then click on the **All Applications** button located on the right-hand side of the **Favorites** pane:

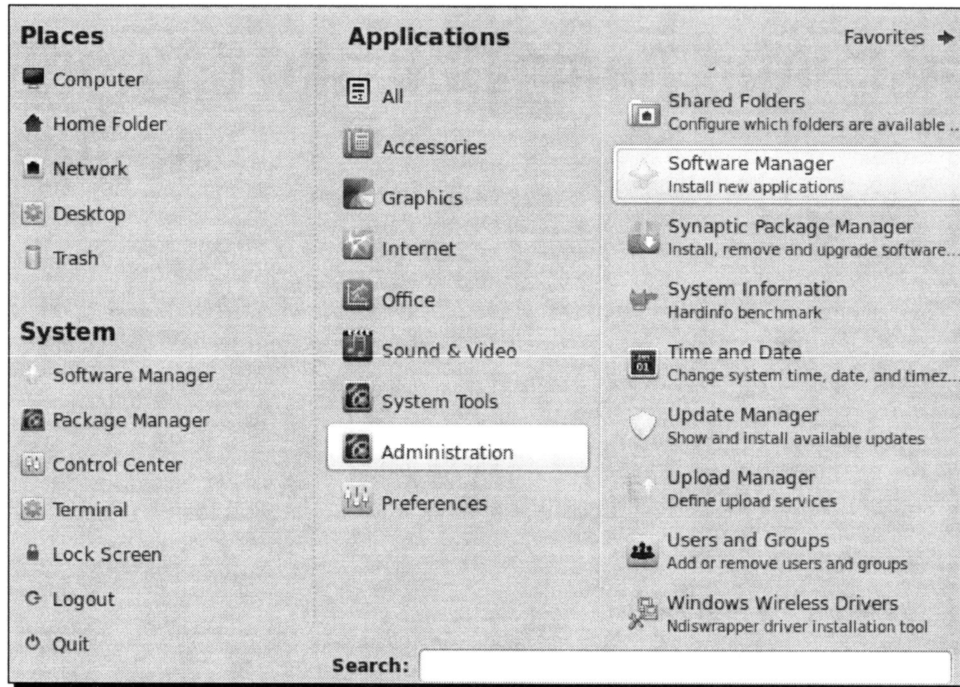

2. Look for the **Administration** menu option, and click on the **Software Manager** menu option; then a new window will be displayed:

3. Enter **abiword** in the textbox located on the right-hand side of the **Software Manager** main window, then hit *Enter* when you're ready.
4. Now, you can see a list with a lot of software that is related to your search. Actually, the first result of the list is the text processor that we want to install, which is shown in the following screenshot:

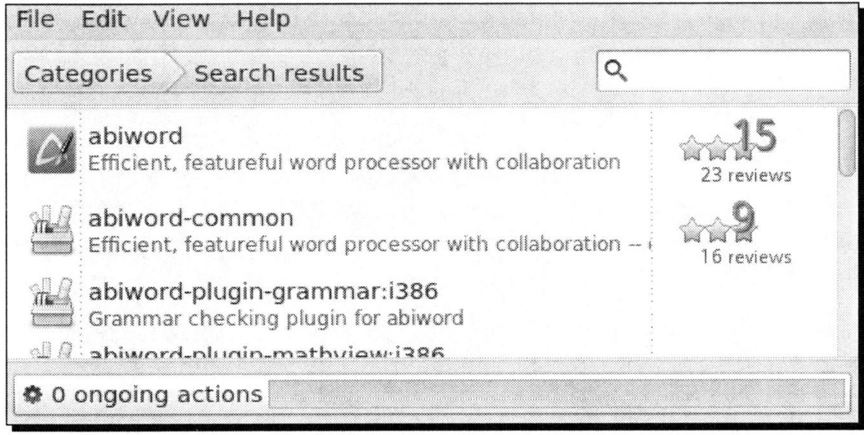

5. Double-clicking on an item will display information about the selected item:

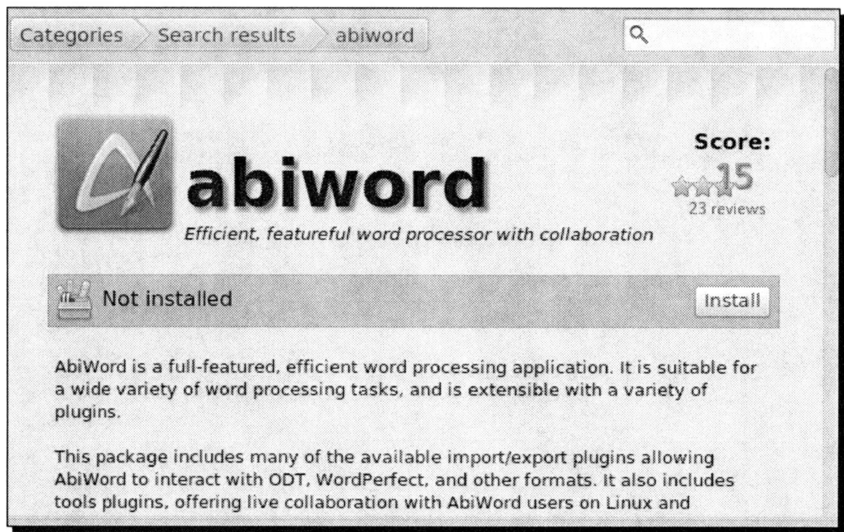

6. Right now, you're ready to click on the **Install** button. By doing that, the installation process for AbiWord will be launched. You can see a progress bar indicating how the installation is progressing.
7. In order to check whether AbiWord is installed in your system, you can open a shell and type `AbiWord`, and then press *Enter*. AbiWord will be executed, and you can start to use it.

What just happened?

Usually, GNU/Linux distributions include a lot of software that is ready to be installed in a specific format called a **package**. Software is organized in different packages and some applications need more than one package; this is known as **package dependency**. Linux Mint uses packages in the **Debian** (**DEB**) format, the same as the Ubuntu Linux and Debian operating systems.

Packages are usually retrieved and installed from a storage location in a computer. This location is called a repository, and it contains many software packages ready to be downloaded and installed in your machine.

Software Manager is an application developed by Linux Mint developers specifically for Linux Mint. This tool allows you to list, install, and remove software. Technically, Software Manager is a frontend for some commands, such as `apt-get` and `apt-cache`. Using a GUI, Software Manager provides an easy and intuitive way to list, install, and remove software, avoiding the use of the command-line interface.

For learning how to install software, we've installed AbiWord, a simple but useful word processor. As you must have discovered, it's pretty easy to install software through packages provided by Linux Mint. You only need to look for some software and click on the **Install** button. Obviously, you can install a lot of different software on your machine following the same process.

It's important to know that not only software distributed in packages can be installed in Linux Mint, but you can install software distributed in other formats, such as tarball and ZIP files as well. However, Mint includes a lot of software distributed in DEB packages, so this method of installation is advisable. Actually, it's good practice to use Software Manager to install software on your Linux Mint operating system.

Have a go hero – discovering software provided by Linux Mint

When you launch Software Manager, a window showing you different icons will be displayed. Each icon represents a different category of software included in Linux Mint. For example, you can see the **Internet**, **Sound and Video**, **Graphics**, and **Office** categories, among others. By clicking on each one, you'll have access to packages belonging to the selected category. You can try and click on a category, take a look at the list of packages for that category, and try to install one of the packages. This process allows you to discover interesting software that can be installed on your machine.

Removing software

Previously, we learned how to install software on your Linux Mint machine. Also, it's interesting and useful to know how to do the opposite step. You can remove installed software on your machine by following a simple process using the Software Manager tool. Remember, you can remove software installed by default during the installation process of the operating system or remove software that you have installed through the Software Manager application.

Time for action – removing the AbiWord program

Let's remove AbiWord from our system by following these steps:

1. Click on the **Menu** button. On the left-hand side of the pane following the **System** label, you will find an option called **Software Manager**. Click on it.
2. Now, **Software Manager** will be launched. Type `abiword` in the search box, and press *Enter*.

3. You will see a list displaying coincidences of your searching; click on the first one, and **Software Manager** will show you some information about **AbiWord**.
4. In order to remove **AbiWord** from your system, you only need to click on the **Remove** button and the removing process will start automatically.

What just happened?

As we have noted before, Software Manager allows us to remove software from our system. We only need to look for the right package, select it, and then click on the **Remove** button. It's an easy and clean process, which helps the system administrators to a great extent. Also, it's very intuitive for newbie users who don't want to use the command-line interface.

Before clicking on the **Remove** button, you can see a label informing you that the AbiWord software was installed on your system. When the software is not installed, this label is different and a **Not Installed** message is displayed instead. This is a simple and effective way to find out whether specific software is installed on your Linux Mint machine.

By now, you must have realized that we launched Software Manager through a different menu option than what was explained previously in the *Installing software* section. Both of them are valid methods for launching this useful tool.

Upgrading software

Between the release cycles, Linux Mint developers upgrade some software that is included in the operating system. This means that the system administrators should check what software has been upgraded and they should decide which software should be installed on the machine. Occasionally, upgraded software only applies minor changes, such as simple improvements or unimportant bug fixes. However, at times upgraded software also includes important security bug fixes. If we don't apply them, our machine could be at serious risk. That's the reason we frequently check which software has been upgraded for our Linux Mint version.

Time for action – upgrading software through the Update Manager tool

Now we're going to find out which software is ready to be upgraded and then proceed to install it:

1. Click on the **Menu** button on the bottom panel, and then click on the **All Applications** button located in the right-hand side of the **Favorites** pane. Now you can see a menu option called **Administration**; click on it to display a new menu, where you can see the **Update Manager** menu option, as shown in the following screenshot:

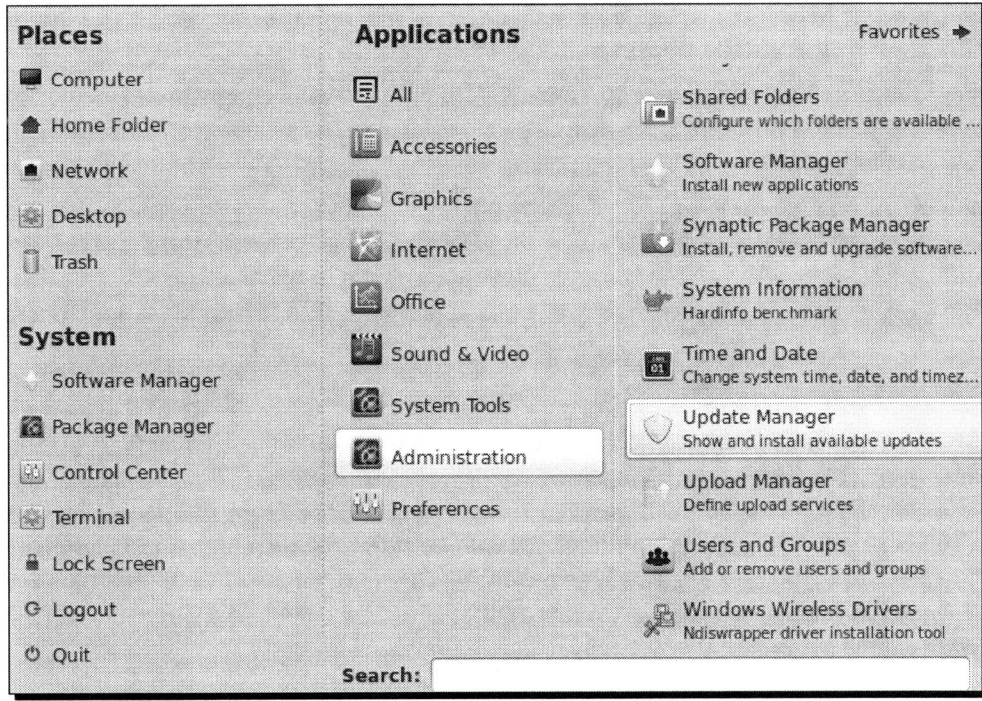

2. After clicking on the **Update Manager** menu option, an application with the same name will be launched, as can been seen here:

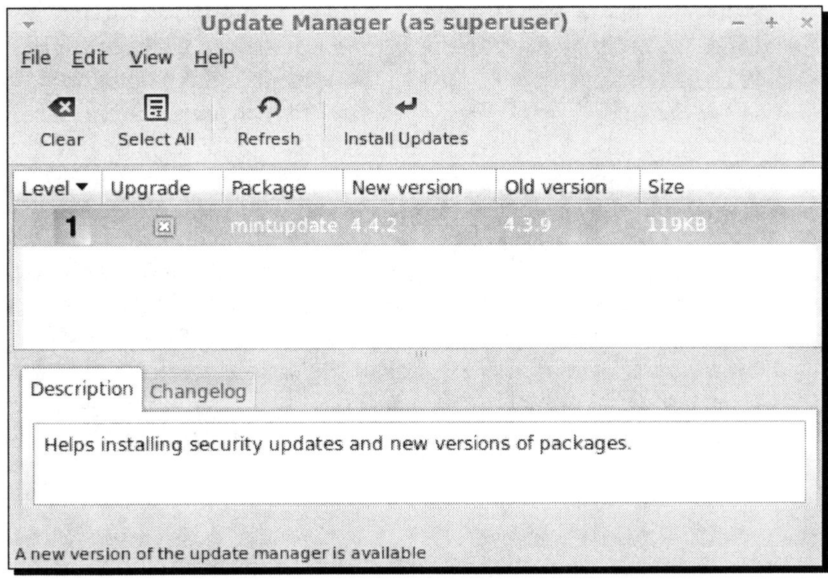

3. **Update Manager** displays a list with only a single package that can be upgraded. Click on the **Install Updates** button.
4. The upgrading process for the **mintupdate** package will be launched; when this process is finished, you will see a complete list of available software that can be upgraded.
5. Right now, you're ready to select the packages that you want to upgrade. It's good practice to select all of them; you should install the packages listed as level **1** at least. Click on the **Install Updates** button when you're ready.
6. When the upgrading process is finished, you'll see an empty list in **Update Manager**.

What just happened?

Update Manager is an effective application provided by Linux Mint to install new versions of installed software and to install security upgrades on your machine. When you launch that application the first time, you will see only a single item in a list for applying upgrades. This item indicates that you need to install an upgrade for **mintupdate**, which is the codename of Update Manager. Obviously, before applying other upgrades, we need to upgrade the tool itself. Once this process is finished, **Update Manager** will be launched again to check which software can be upgraded.

The list of software ready to be upgraded displays different items, providing information about the package name, installed version, and new version available. Also, a number for each item is displayed. This number ranges from 1 to 5, and it indicates a level based on the importance of the upgrade. Level 1 indicates that Linux Mint developers certify that a package and packages marked with this level should be upgraded as soon as possible. Usually, security updates use this level. The next level is for those packages whose upgrade is recommended by Linux Mint developers. Level 3 indicates that it is safe to apply an upgrade, but Linux Mint developers didn't test it. Packages marked with level 4 are unsafe, and if you upgrade them, the stability of the system can be affected. Finally, level 5 is for dangerous packages (in the unstable stage of development or with broken dependencies), and Linux Mint developers know that they can damage the operating system.

In general terms, it's a good idea to launch Software Manager frequently and upgrade only those packages marked as level 1 and level 2. For levels 3, 4, and 5, system administrators and advanced users should decide whether to upgrade. Also, you can mark all the packages listed or only a few of them. Usually, this is a task of the system administrator; it is he or she who takes these kinds of decisions. By default, only packages from level 1 to 3 are displayed in the list for upgrading. You can change this preference by going to **Edit** | **Preferences**.

Have a go hero – finding out how to change preferences in Update Manager

Some preferences of Update Manager can be changed. For example, you can change which level of upgrade is displayed by default. Also, you can select the frequency for refreshing information after clicking on the **Refresh** button. On the other hand, you can decide which packages will be ignored by Update Manager.

Another important option offered by Update Manager is the option of choosing which kind of packages can be installed and from what server. By default, main, upstream, and imported packages are selected. Also, it's possible to add additional repositories instead of the official ones provided by Mint. For the server, the main server of Linux Mint is selected, but you can choose one of the many available mirrors.

Summary

After reading this chapter, you have learned how to deal with software on your computer. Basically, we have discovered how to perform some important operations, such as installing, removing, and upgrading software. Linux Mint offers us two great applications to carry out these actions related to software, namely Update Manager and Software Manager.

Specifically, we covered:

- How Linux Mint distributes software using packages
- Using Software Manager to add and remove software on Linux Mint
- How to upgrade software through the Update Manager tool

Although Software Manager is the main tool for installing and removing software in Linux Mint, another tool called **Synaptic Package Manager** is included in this operating system. This tool offers a low-level control of packages, so you can use it when you're looking for a specific package instead of a specific application. Remember that a single application can be distributed in more than one package.

In the next chapter, we're going to learn how to deal with hardware in Linux Mint.

6

Configuring Hardware

Your computer includes and uses different hardware and peripherals such as a processor, keyboard, monitor, graphical card, and a sound card. When these devices are working properly, your computer works without any hardware problems. In this chapter, we're going to learn how to configure the hardware of your computer.

We shall cover the following topics in this chapter:

- How to detect hardware
- Configuring your monitor
- How to configure your keyboard and mouse
- Configuring sound
- How to install additional drivers

Detecting hardware

Before proceeding to configure your hardware, it's important to find out which devices are working within your computer. Linux Mint offers a graphical tool to get information about the hardware installed on your computer. Also, we're going to learn how to use commands to display low-level information about devices using USB and PCI interfaces.

Time for action – how to display the device information

Let's display information about devices running on your computer:

1. Click on the **Menu** button from the bottom panel and then click on the **Control Center** menu option belonging to the **System** group, as shown in the following screenshot:

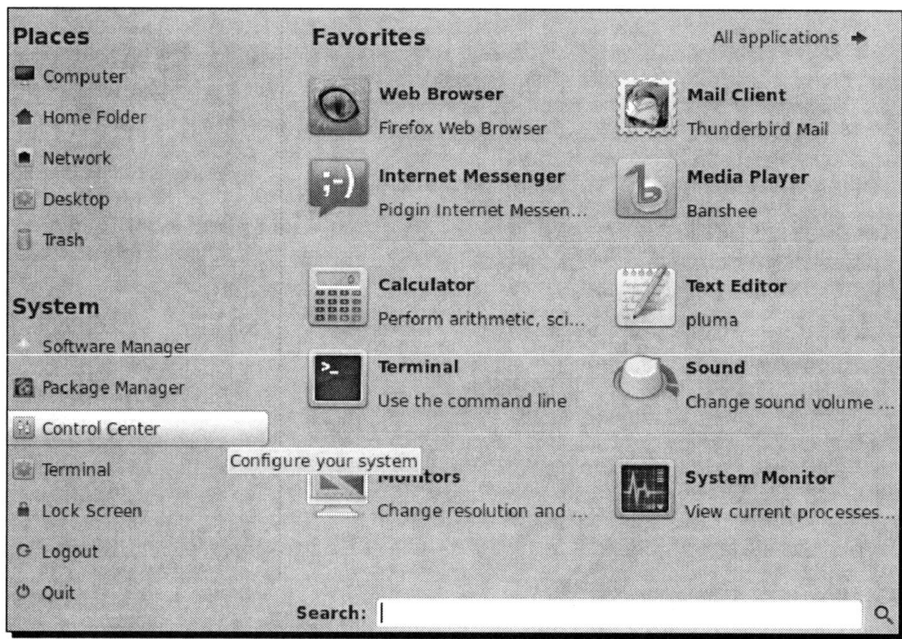

2. Now you can see a new window; click on the **Hardware** menu option:

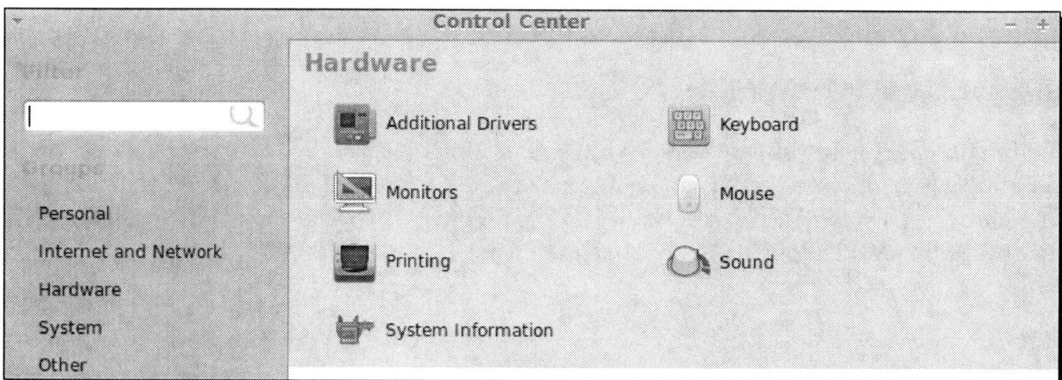

3. Click on the **System Information** link, you'll then see a new window, which belongs to an application called **HardInfo**.
4. On the left-hand side pane of the main window, you'll find a tree structure where the **Devices** icon gives you access to information about hardware installed on your computer, as shown in the following screenshot:

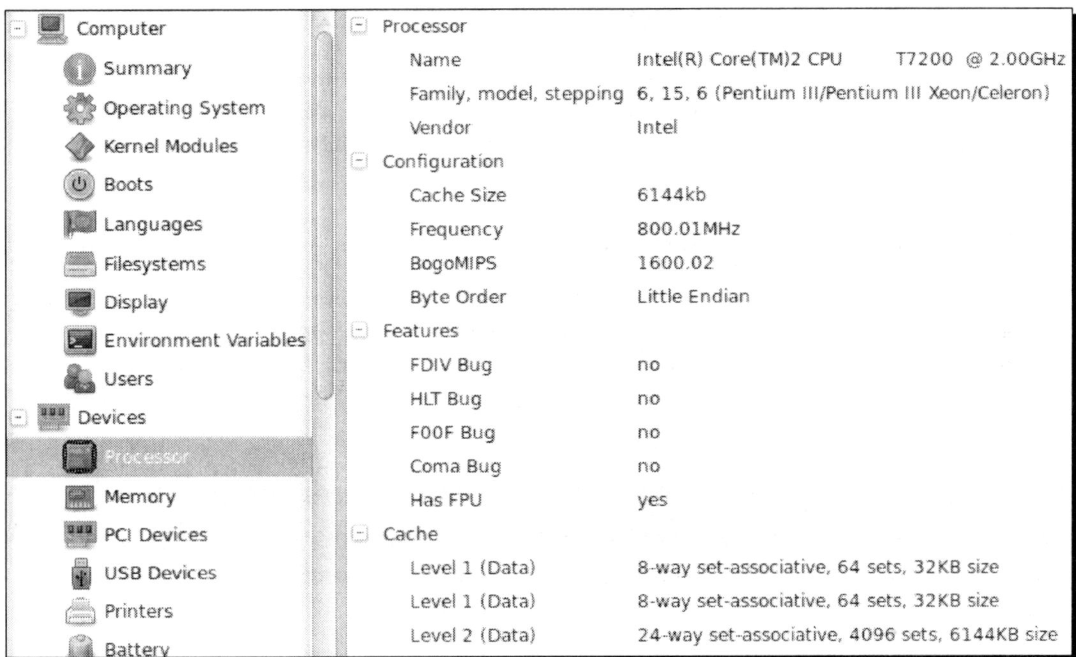

What just happened?

Linux Mint included HardInfo for displaying information about the hardware installed on your computer. You can see information about many devices, such as a processor, memory, printers, and USB devices connected to your computer. Also, HardInfo offers you other relevant information about environment variables, users, or kernel modules loaded during boot time.

If you need to get any information provided by HardInfo in HTML or text format, you can do this through the **Generate Report** button. This report can be very useful to share information about the hardware installed on your computer.

On the other hand, HardInfo is accessible through **Control Center**, a software tool that provides you access to many useful applications for configuring different aspects of your operating system.

Have a go hero – using the dmesg, lspci, and lsusb commands

Although HardInfo is a very intuitive and easy-to-use tool, you also can use other commands to get information about hardware installed on your computer. For example, `dmesg` is a command that prints on the shell information provided by the kernel. This means that if a USB device is connected to your computer, the Linux kernel will produce information about this; so `dmesg` will retrieve this kind of information.

In order to get data about the USB devices connected to your computer, you can execute the `lsusb` command. If you want to get information about your PCI devices, the `lspci` command can be used, as it provides you with a complete list of the required information.

Configuring your monitor

Monitors are one of the most important peripherals of your computer. Thanks to your monitor, you can see all your information and data displayed for your computer. Several monitors allow you to change some properties, such as screen resolution, rotation, and refresh rate. We're going to learn how to change some of these properties through a graphical tool provided by Linux Mint.

Time for action – changing the screen resolution

Although you can change many different properties of your monitor, now we'll look at how to change screen resolution:

1. Launch the **Control Center** application, and click on the **Monitors** link.
2. Go to the **Resolution** option, and choose the appropriate resolution for your monitor; a sample is shown in the following screenshot:

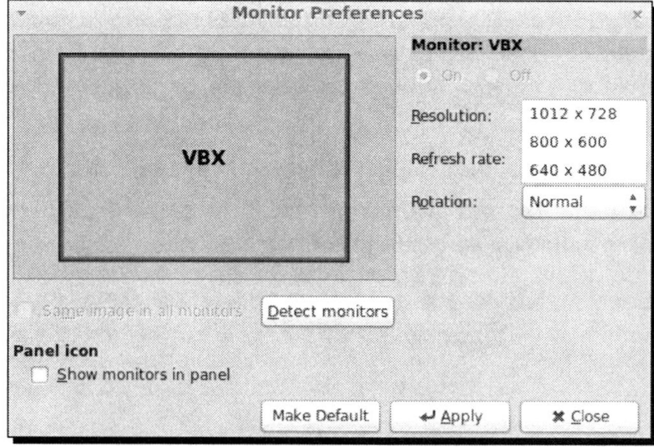

3. Click on the **Apply** button when you're done.

What just happened?

It's pretty easy to change some of the properties of your monitor, thanks to the graphic tool provided by Mint. You've learned how to change the resolution of your screen; along with this, you can also change the rotation and refresh rate of your monitor. Also, it's possible to detect which monitor or monitors are connected to your computer. Based on this detection, Mint can automatically select a better resolution for those monitor/monitors. If you have connected multiple monitors, Mint allows you to configure each of them without any problems. Don't forget to click on the **Apply** button after changing the properties, otherwise your changes won't be applied.

Configuring a keyboard

In the previous section, you learned how to configure your monitor, now it's time for another important peripheral—your keyboard. Linux Mint allows you to choose a specific keyboard brand and model; it also adds different layouts and configures your keyboard for getting accessibility. In this section, we're going to learn how to add a new layout.

Time for action – adding a new layout

Let's figure out how to add a Spanish layout to your keyboard:

1. Launch **Control Center,** and click on the **Keyboard** button.
2. Click on the **Layouts** tab, which is shown in the following screenshot:

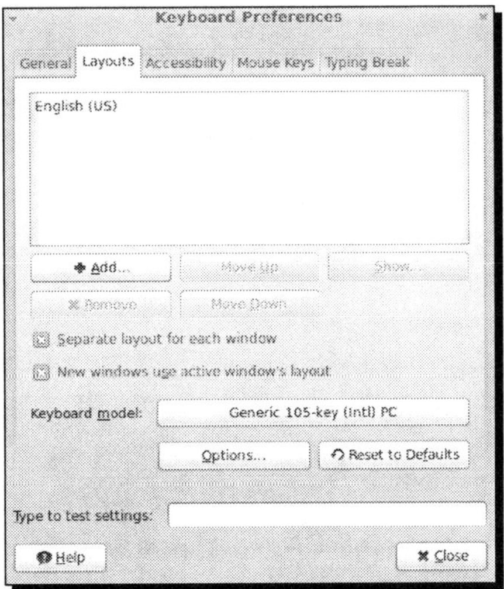

3. Click on the **Add...** button.
4. Now, click on the **By language** tab.
5. Look for the **Spanish; Castilian** option, and select it for the **Language** drop-down menu, as shown in the following screenshot:

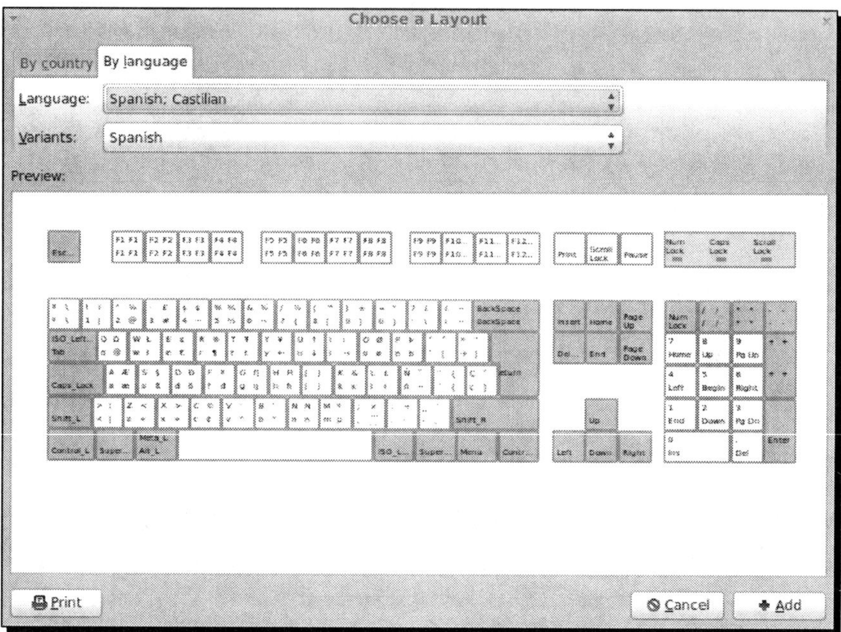

6. Click on the **Add** button when you're done.
7. Now you have a **Spanish** layout available for your keyboard, as shown in the following screenshot:

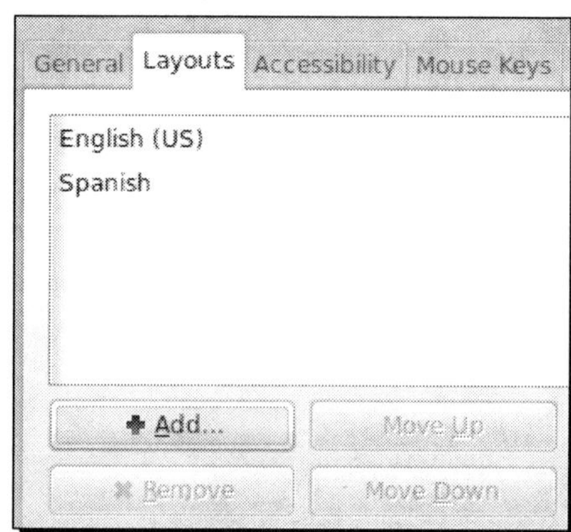

What just happened?

Some users would want to use a different layout for their keyboard. For example, there may be some developers whose mother tongue is not English, but they prefer to use this kind of layout for programming. However, they need to use another different layout for writing in languages such as French or Spanish. Only a single layout can be selected at a time, but users can change their layouts at any time. Keep in mind that you must add a new layout before using it.

In addition to configuring the layout for your keyboard, you can also configure different aspects such as the brand and model of your keyboard, or decide if the cursor should blink or not in text fields. Changing these properties is easy, thanks to the graphic tool provided by Linux Mint.

Configuring your mouse

In the preceding sections, we've learned how to configure our monitor and our keyboard, but we have another important peripheral that allows us to communicate with our computer. We're talking about the mouse. Mint provides a simple and easy-to-use tool to change properties of your mouse.

Time for action – changing mouse orientation

Let's learn how to change the orientation of the mouse from right-hand to left-hand:

1. Again, we'll launch the **Control Center** application, and click on the **Keyboard** button on the **Hardware** group.
2. Select the **Left-handed** option on the **Mouse Orientation** group.
3. Click on the **Close** button when you're done.

What just happened?

Although we explained a simple example of configuring the mouse, Mint allows you to change additional properties, such as the pointer speed, timeout for double-clicking, or showing the position of the mouse pointer when the *Ctrl* key is pressed. Also, it's possible to configure your mouse for better accessibility.

Configuring sound

If your computer includes a sound card, you can configure the behavior of sound in your machine. Mint offers you a graphic tool to change and configure many aspects related to the sound, such as output volume, sound effects, kind of sound for alerts, and enable or disable sound for windows and buttons. In order to get familiar with how to configure sound, we're going to learn how to enable sound for windows and buttons.

Time for action – how to enable window and button sound

Let's look at how to enable sound for windows and buttons using the graphic tool included in Linux Mint:

1. Launch **Control Center**.
2. Click on the **Sound** button, after which you see a contextual menu; click on the **Start Sound** option.
3. Now, you can access the **Sound Preferences** window; check the **Enable window and buttons sound** checkbox.
4. Click on the **Close** button to finish the **Sound Preferences** application.

What just happened?

The **Sound Preferences** window allows you to configure many sound-related aspects. Using this window, we learned how to enable sound for windows and buttons. In addition to that, you can use this window to change volume for the output, use the mute function to disable all sounds, or to decide which applications are going to use sounds.

Installing additional drivers

During the installation process, Linux Mint detects your hardware and installs the required drivers for it. Some GNU/Linux distributions don't install or provide the proprietary drivers; however, Mint offers us the option to install these kinds of drivers. This is a good idea, because it makes life easier for novice users. The goal is to get all hardware working inside your computer, including multimedia support, monitors, and graphic cards.

Modern PCs include graphic cards manufactured from different brands that need proprietary drivers. If manufactures release source code, it's possible to compile it and to generate binary packages. This is part of the job of Mint developers, who provide software to allow us to use our computer with Linux Mint out of the box.

You can check if Mint provides additional drivers for your hardware. In order to do that, you can access **Control Center,** and click on the **Additional Drivers** button. Then a search process will start and Mint will inform you which additional drivers can be installed.

Summary

In this chapter, we talked about how to detect and configure the hardware of your computer. We provided simple examples of configurations, but it's easy to configure devices such as keyboard, mouse, and monitors thanks to the graphic tools included in Linux Mint.

Specifically, we covered the following topics:

- Detecting hardware attached to your computer
- Configuring important peripherals such as a keyboard, monitor, and mouse
- Configuring sound
- Installing additional drivers

The community website of Linux Mint provides complete information about which hardware is compatible with this distribution of GNU/Linux. This resource is known as *Hardware Database* and it's accessible at `http://community.linuxmint.com/hardware`. You can look for hardware based on the level of compatibility, brand, type, or Mint releases.

In the next chapter, we're going to learn how to deal with networking in Linux Mint.

7

Networking

Nowadays, computers work together through network-sharing resources such as files, folders, and printers. In fact, the Internet is a huge network where computers are working to exchange data. In this chapter, you'll learn how to carry out some basic system administrator tasks related to networking.

In this chapter, we will cover about the following topics:

- Configuring wired and wireless networks
- Accessing Window's shared folders
- Connecting to servers through the FTP protocol

Configuring a wired network

Although wireless networks are very extended, a lot of companies and universities still use a wired computer network. We're going to learn how to configure our computer to access a local network, and also access the Internet. Keep in mind that before accessing the Internet from a local network, you need to access the network itself.

Time for action – configuring your connection

Let's say we want to connect our computer to a local network using a static IP of `192.168.1.45`. We know that the DNS server is using `8.8.8.8` as an IP address. Also, our gateway can be reached at `192.168.1.125`. Perform the following steps to configure your connection:

1. Launch the **Control Center** tool from the main menu.
2. Click on the **Network** button inside the **Internet and Network** group.
3. Now you have access to a window called **Network Settings**.
4. Click on the **Click to make changes** button.
5. Before continuing to the next step, you should be authenticated. So, you need to enter your password and click on the **Authenticate** button when you're ready. The first tab, called **Connections**, has an option named **Wired connection**; click on it, as shown in the following screenshot:

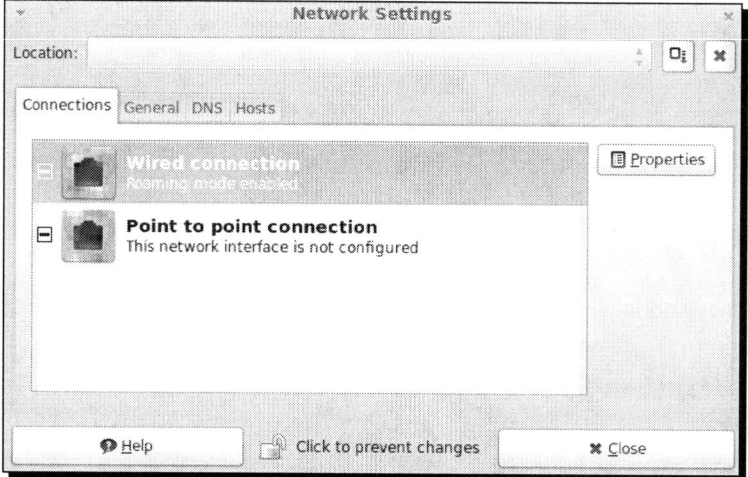

6. Click on the **Properties** button of the **Network Settings** window.
7. Select **Static IP address** from the **Configuration** drop-down menu and enter **192.168.1.45** in the **IP address** input box. After that, the input box loses focus and the **Subnet mask** input box will be filled automatically. Enter **192.168.1.125** in the **Gateway address** input box. All these settings are shown in the following screenshot:

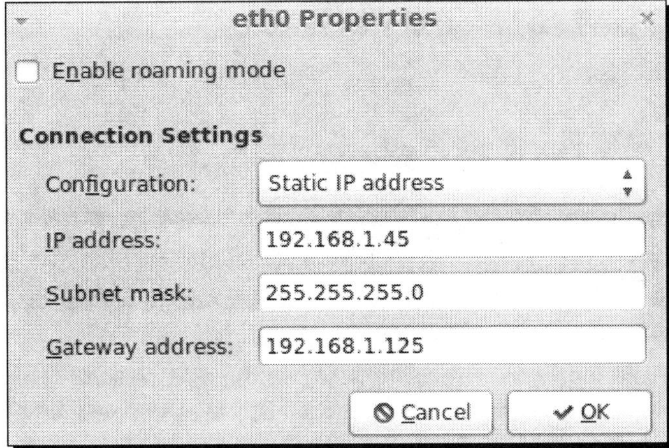

8. Click on the **OK** button when you're done.
9. Click on the **DNS** tab, and click on the **Add** button. Now, you can enter `8.8.8.8` in the first input box. Click on the **Close** button when you're ready; your network is now configured.

What just happened?

We have learned how to connect to a local network through a simple GUI application included in Linux Mint. Although some system administrators prefer to use the command-line interface, it's pretty easy and intuitive to use this graphical interface.

In our example, we configured our network card, assigning it a static IP address and setting a gateway and a specific server as **Domain Name Server** (**DNS**). The functionality of this kind of server is very important, because it resolves domain names into an IP address.

Although the **Network Settings** application automatically configures the subnet mask, you can also add your own data. Note that the subnet mask is calculated based on the IP address that you have entered.

Some networks use automatic configuration based on **Dynamic Host Configuration Protocol** (**DHCP**) instead of using static IP addresses. In that case, you can configure your network access by selecting **Automatic configuration (DHCP) for Configuration** from the drop-down menu.

Have a go hero – changing the hostname

If you want, it's possible to change your hostname. You need to use the same application that you used for configuring your network. Simply access the **General** tab and enter your new hostname in the **Host name** input box.

Configuring the wireless network

Nowadays, wireless networks are very popular; companies, universities, airports, and coffee shops use this kind of network to establish connections to the Internet. We will learn how to configure your Linux Mint computer to use a wireless network.

Time for action – how to connect your computer to a wireless network

Imagine we need to connect our computer to a wireless network that is using **Testing** as **SSID** and the **WEP-128** method for security. Also, we're going to use the same data for the **IP address**, **Subnet mask**, and **Gateway address** input boxes as we used when we configured our network in the previous section.

1. Launch the **Control Center** tool from the main menu.
2. Click on the **Network Connections** option from the **Other** group.
3. Click on the **Wireless** tab, and then click on the **Add** button.
4. Now you have a new window where you can add your configuration data. Choose a name for your connection, add **Testing** to the **SSID** input box, and click on the **Save...** button when you're ready, as shown in the following screenshot:

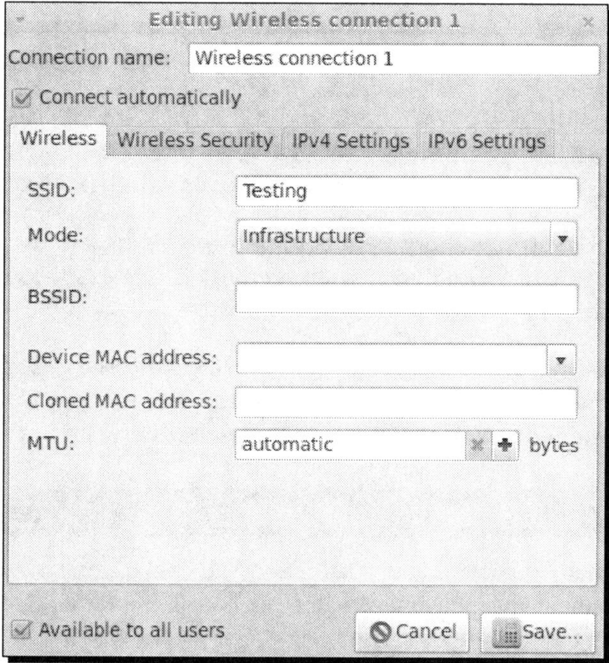

5. Click on the **Wireless Security** tab and choose **WEP 128-bit Passphrase** from the **Security** drop-down menu. Inside the **Key** textbox, enter `MyKey`. If you want to make sure what you are entering is correct, check the **Show key** checkbox:

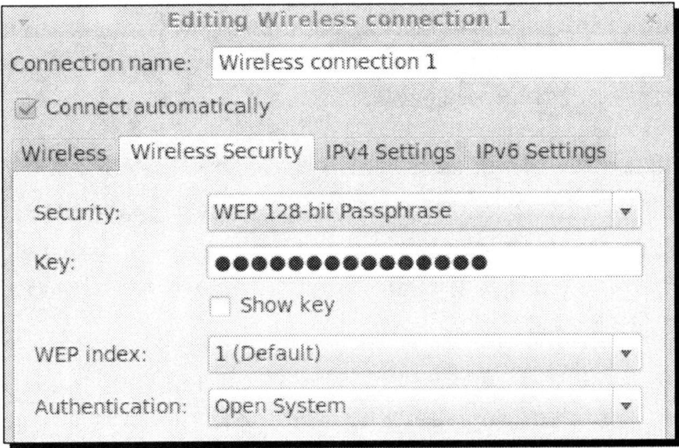

6. Now it's time for setting your IP properties. Click on the **Add** button and enter `192.168.1.45` for the **IP address** input box, `255.255.255.0` for the **Subnet mask** input box, and `192.168.1.125` for the **Gateway address** input box.

7. Click on the **Save...** button. Your wireless network is now configured.

What just happened?

Mint offers us a simple but effective graphic tool to configure our wireless connection. You've learned how to do that using manual configuration for your IP address, subnet mask, and gateway. Also, our example used the **WEP 128-bit** method for security. This method needs a key, which we need to type. If the network that you are trying to configure is using a different security method, you can select it accordingly. Other available methods for security are **WEP 40/128-bit**, **LEAP**, **dynamic WEP**, and **WPA**.

On the other hand, similar to a wired network, you can use DHCP instead of a manual configuration. It depends on your wireless network.

By now, you must have noticed that inside the configuration window there exists a marked option that allows you to connect automatically to the wireless network. Thanks to this option, your computer will be connected to the wireless network every time it boots.

If your computer has a wireless card, Mint will try to autodetect, by default, which wireless networks are available. You can configure your connection by choosing any one of them.

Accessing a Windows-shared folder

It is very useful to share resources such as folders, files, and printers inside a computer network. Usually, computers in the same network may be using different operating systems. Since Windows is one of the most widely used operating systems, more than one computer inside your network can use it. Keeping this in mind, it could be very useful to know how to access a Windows-shared folder from Linux.

Time for action – how to access a specific shared folder

We're going to access a shared folder called `windows_shared`, which exists in a Windows 7 computer and is accessible from your Linux Mint computer over the network. This is how we can access a specific shared folder:

1. In your Linux Mint desktop, you can see an icon depicted as a labeled folder, indicating that this icon represents your home folder. This icon gives you access to **Caja**, the Linux Mint file manager. For example, if your username is **john**, the icon label would be **john's Home**.
2. Caja is now opened and you can see an icon with the **Network** label; click on it.
3. At this point, you should see an icon that represents a Windows PC. This icon will use a label with the name of the Windows hostname's computer. Click on it to access the shared folders. For example, in the following screenshot, it is named **AL-PC**:

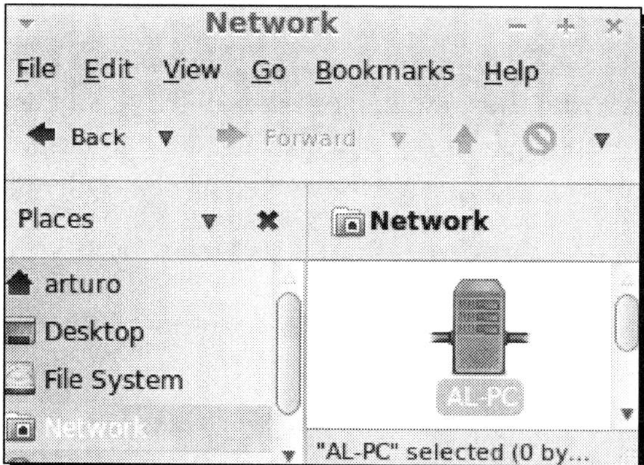

4. A new dialog window, asking you about your username, password, and domain, will be now displayed. Enter your data and click on the **Connect** button when you're ready.
5. Now, the **windows_shared** folder will be available in the Windows manager. You can now double-click on it to access the files inside it.

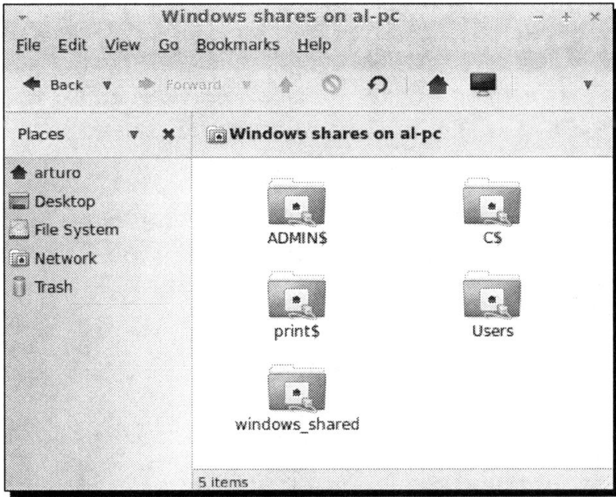

What just happened?

Thanks to Samba, it is now possible to access shared folders in Windows from Linux. From a technical point of view, Samba is a free reimplementation of the **SMB/CIFS** networking protocol. This protocol operates as an application-layer network and is used by Windows for sharing files, printers, and other resources.

Obviously, before accessing the Windows-shared folders from Linux, you need to know some important information, such as workgroup, username, and password. This data should be provided by the Windows system administrator.

By default, Linux Mint explores your network to discover which computers are accessible. This happens when you click on the **Network** button of Caja. When your Windows computer is detected and you click on its icon, you can enter your data to access these shared folders. Then, you can work with the files inside this folder as if they were locally inside your computer.

Remember that, by default, all shared folders will be displayed on Caja after authentication. However, you can only access those folders with permissions from a user who is connected to a Windows PC.

Connecting to servers

It's very common for servers on the Internet to provide access to other servers and computers by using different network protocols. **FTP**, **SSH**, and **WebDAV** are common protocols to access remote servers, so it would be very helpful to know how to connect with other computers from Linux Mint using these protocols.

Time for action – connecting to an FTP server

We're going to connect to a public FTP server, which provides access to Linux kernel resources. It can be reached at `ftp.kernel.org`; we don't need any username or password to access it.

1. Open the Caja file manager by clicking on the **Home Folder** option, which is accessible through the main menu, in the **Places** group.
2. Go to the **File** menu, and click on **Connect to server**.
3. A new dialog will be displayed. Choose **Public FTP** from the **Service** drop-down menu. Enter **ftp.kernel.org** in the **Server** textbox as shown in the following screenshot:

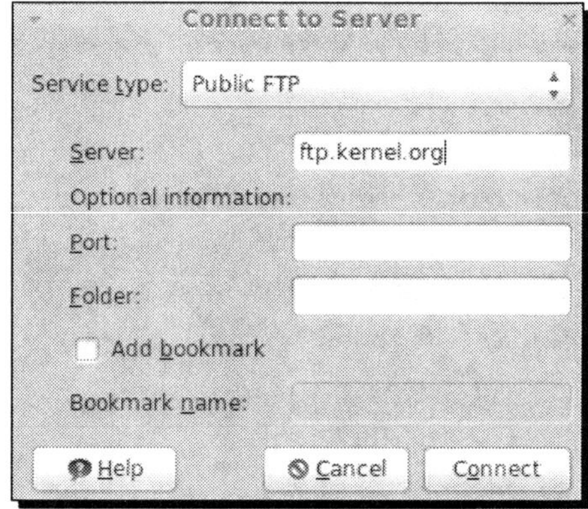

4. You can see all the available folders through the FTP server in your file manager window, as shown here:

What just happened?

The Caja file manager helps us connect to servers using different network protocols. In our example, we've learned how to connect to a public FTP server. This kind of server doesn't need a username and password combination. If you need to connect to one of these servers, you can choose the **FTP (with login)** option from the **Service** drop-down menu. Once the connection is established, you can access the files and folders through Caja as if they were in your computer. This means you can copy content directly from another file manager window using the drag-and-drop technique.

Inside the connection dialog, you can see that an option called **Add bookmark exists**. By selecting that option, a shortcut will be created in your file manager. Thanks to this functionality, you can quickly access your most common server connections.

Have a go hero – connecting to a server using the secure WebDAV protocol

Try connecting to a server through the secure WebDAV protocol. You can follow the same steps as explained before for connecting to a public FTP server. We only need to select **Secure WebDAV (HTTPS)** from the **Security** drop-down menu. Also, you can enter your username for the server, and the default folder name where the connection will be established.

Summary

We learned a lot in this chapter about how to perform some basic networking operations.

Specifically, we covered the following topics:

- Connecting to wired and wireless networks
- Accessing remote computers using the FTP and WebDAV protocols
- Connecting to a Windows-shared folder

Now that you know how to deal with networks, it's time to learn about the different types of available filesystems and how to make and restore backups.

8

Storage and Backup

This chapter covers basic concepts and information about filesystems, storage types, and how to create and restore backups. System administrators should have a deep knowledge of these topics as this information is of huge value to users, companies, universities, and other kinds of organizations.

In this chapter, we shall cover the following topics:

- Finding out the main filesystem types used by GNU/Linux distributions
- How to assign disk quota to users
- How to analyze your disk usage
- How to create and restore backups

Filesystem types

Computer data is stored and organized in a specific system in storage devices. The operating system should be able to store, organize, access, and update that data. In order to execute all these operations, a **filesystem** is used. All files and folders inside a storage device are organized by a filesystem, and the operating system deals with it. A storage device can be a hard drive, an external USB drive, or a set of files and folders on a network.

Each filesystem offers the system administrators and users a set of metadata to work with it. This metadata includes information such as length of a data contained in a file, the owner of a file, and the time that the file was last modified. Currently, you can find a lot of filesystems, and each family of operating systems is able to work with many of them. The Linux kernel is the main component of the operating system that deals directly with filesystems. Also, Linux distributions offer tools and techniques to work with different types of filesystems.

Filesystems and storage devices use the concept of **partition**, which identifies a slice of a storage device used by a filesystem. Usually, each storage device is divided by partitions, and each of them can be formatted using a specific filesystem. A formatting operation provides a mechanism to create a filesystem inside a partition. Remember that Mint automatically creates some partitions in our hard drive during the installation process.

Mint allows us to work with some of the most popular filesystems used by the Linux operating system family. Specifically, Linux Mint can work with partitions such as `ext2`, `ext3`, `ext4`, `btrfs`, `xfs`, and `reiserfs`. Currently, `ext4` is a standard de facto for Linux partitions, and Linux Mint uses it by default. Although `btrfs` is experimental, you can test it in your hard drive, thanks to Mint. On the other hand, `reiserfs` is very popular for its journaled features and its stability. Some system administrators prefer to use `xfs` due to its high-performance journaled system.

Decisions about which is the best filesystem type for each computer and storage device are not trivial. Usually, system administrators prefer to use `ext4` for PC and workstations; `xfs` and `reiserfs` are common for servers and for devices that need high availability and performance.

Related to filesystems, we need to consider: **storages types**. In servers running GNU/Linux operating systems, it is common to use storage types such as **Redundant Array of Independent Disks** (**RAID**) and **Logical Volume Management** (**LVM**). The first one is a technology that basically combines multiple disks into a unique logic unit. Different levels of RAID can be applied; popular choices are RAID 5 and RAID 1. Some advantages of RAID usage are redundancy of data and a high level of performance.

On the other hand, LVM is a method of allocating spaces in storage devices in a more convenient and flexible way using traditional partitions. Using LVM, it is possible to create backups by taking snapshots. In addition to this important feature, LVM allows system administrators to apply hot swapping for adding or replacing disks without disrupting services provided by the device storage. During the installation process Mint allows you to use LVM instead of partitions.

Disk quotas

Hard drives and storage in general have limited space, so it's important to do some tasks of maintenance to prevent those devices from reaching their maximum capacity. An easy way to manage limits on storage is to use **disk quotas**; this is a technique of assigning a specific size space for each user or group of the operating system.

Linux kernel allows us to use two types of quotas for disks: **soft** and **hard**. On using the soft quota , the user will receive a warning when the limit is reached. On the other hand, a hard quota doesn't allow a user to create files after reaching the limit.

Time for action – assigning disk quota to a specific user

We're going to learn how to set a limit of 20 MB for the `/dev/sda3` partition of a specific hard drive for a user called `arturo`. Let's imagine that the `/home` partition is mounted on `/dev/sda3`. The quota assigned to a user will be soft, so a warning message will be received. Obviously, you can choose a different user and partition for your hard drive or other device accessible through your computer.

1. Go to **Menu** and launch the **Software Manager** application, then look for and install an application called **quota**.

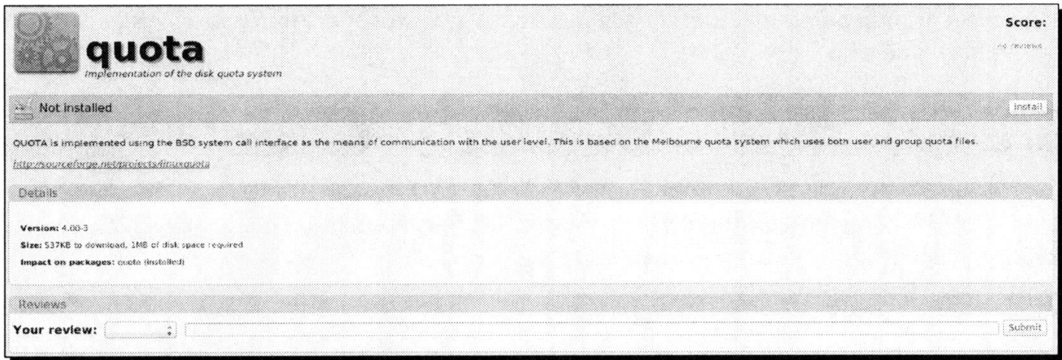

2. Enable quota checking on the filesystem by modifying the `/etc/fstab` file and adding `usrquota` and `grquota` values to a specific partition. Only the root user has permissions to modify the mentioned file, so you need to log in as `root` before changing it. The line in the `/etc/fstab` file should be the following one:

```
/dev/sda3   /home   ext4   defaults,usrquota,grpquota   1 2
```

3. After editing and changing the `/etc/fstab` file, you must reboot your computer.

4. Execute the following command to check the partition where quota has been enabled:

```
$ quotacheck -avug
```

5. Let's assign a quota to our user. In order to do that, you need to execute the next command, which will open an editor to modify a specific configuration file for assigning quotas:

```
$ edquota arturo
```

6. Right now, you can modify the opened file by adding the value `20480` to the **soft** column in the line corresponding to the `/dev/sda3` partition. Save the file when you're ready. Disk quota has now been assigned to the user `arturo`.

What just happened?

The quota application contains two useful commands (`quotacheck` and `edquota`) for setting and checking quotas in hard drives for users and groups. In our example, we've configured our system to launch a warning when a specific user is trying to use more than 20 MB in the `/home` partition.

All information about the partitions that are going to be mounted when a computer boots can be found in the `/etc/fstab` file, which has been modified to activate quota checking. Instead of rebooting the computer, you can unmount and mount the specific partition.

We've just used a limit of 20 MB to check out how a warning message is displayed. Obviously, system administrators choose different values for specific purposes, as each scenario is different.

Have a go hero – scheduling quota checking

You can check periodically whether quota has been reaching the storage limit by using the `quotacheck` command through the `cron` tool. We only need to create a file `/etc/cron.daily/quotacheck` with the following line:

```
quotacheck -avug
```

Thanks to `cron`, the operating system checks each day whether the quota has been reached for each configured user.

Disk usage analysis

We've learned how to assign quotas to users and to preserve space in hard drives. Regarding this functionality, it's important to know how much space is used in each partition and directory. Thanks to this feature, a system administrator can decide how to organize partitions upon disk usage.

Time for action – examining disk usage

We're going to take a look at our hard drive to discover how much space is used for each partition and directory:

1. Go to the main menu and click on the **Disk Usage Analyzer** menu option, which belongs to the **System tools** menu group.
2. Now you have access to a new window, which displays graphic information about your hard drive space and usage:

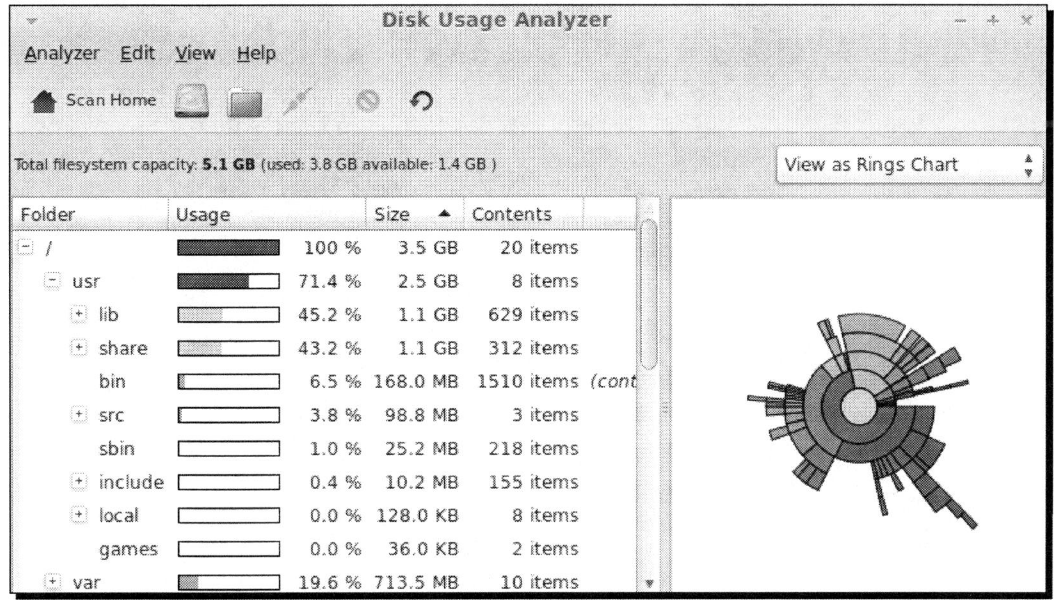

What just happened?

Baobab is the name of the tool used to analyze disk usage provided by Linux Mint. It offers us graphical information about the filesystem capacity and the way in which space is distributed along the hard drive. For each directory in your `home` folder, you can see a number of files, space in percentage, and size. Also, it's possible to choose information about a specific folder, which can be selected through the folder icon located in the main toolbar of Baobab.

Regarding graphical information displayed by Baobab, we can select between two kinds of charts: **treemap** and **rings**. Below the toolbar, a simple line informs us about the capacity of the filesystem and how much space is available. This is a simple but very practical information.

Creating backups

Some information stored on computers is very important and valuable, so we need to keep it safe. Also, it's recommended to make backups, so that if some of this information is lost or damaged, we can restore the backup, and everything should work properly again. Let's learn how to create backups from Linux Mint.

Time for action – making a backup of a specific folder

We're going to make a backup of a folder called `testbackup`, which is inside your `home` folder, to a folder called `backup` inside the `/tmp` directory. You can create the `testbackup` folder and add some files inside it.

1. Click on **Menu** and then click again on the **All Applications** option, and choose **Backup Tool** inside the **Administration** group.
2. The **Backup Tool** application will be launched and you can see a new window with a few buttons. Click on the **Backup files** button:

3. Choose the **testbackup** folder for the **Source** option and select the **backup** folder from the **/tmp** folder for the **Destination** drop-down option. Click on the **Forward** button when you're ready:

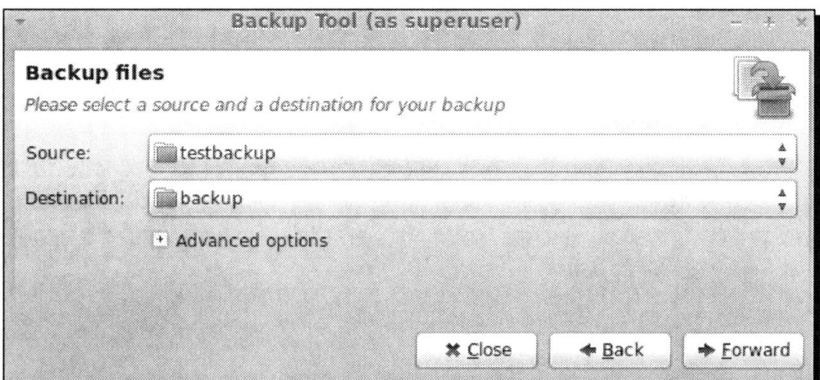

4. The next options allow you to exclude some folders and directories. We're not going to exclude anything, so you can click on the **Forward** button.
5. Review your source and destination folders. If everything is fine, then click **Apply**.
6. Finally, you can see a message informing you about the success of the backup operation. Click on the **Close** button when you're ready. Take a look at the `backup` folder to make sure your files are there.

What just happened?

Backup Tool is an application included in Linux Mint that provides a simple and effective way to make and restore backups of files, folders, and applications. We've explained a basic operation—how to make a backup of a folder. However, Backup Tool also allows you to create a backup of a simple file or even some applications installed on your computer.

Advanced options provided by Backup Tool allow us to choose an output format and options to perform overwrite, preserve permissions, and timestamp, follow symlinks, or confirm integrity of files and folders. We used the default options, but you can choose your own preferences too.

If you access the `/tmp/backup` folder, you can find files created from Backup Tool. These files will be identical to your files inside the `testbackup` folder.

Apart from choosing a folder inside the same hard disk, you also can make a back up using different devices such as USB pen drives, an external USB disk, or a folder accessible through your network.

Keep in mind that Backup Tool is executed through a root user, so you can backup any directory of your hard drive. Also, you should be authenticated before using this tool.

Have a go hero – creating and restoring a backup file

You can try to create a `tarball` (created with the `tar` utility) file and restore it. As source, you can use a few files instead of a whole directory. Backup Tool offers you the chance to do that with a few clicks. Don't forget to choose the **.tar.gz file** option for the **Output** drop-down option inside **Advanced options**.

Restoring backups

Once you have made backups of your important files, folders, or applications, you should store them in a safe place. If something goes wrong, you can restore these backups in selected files or folders of your hard drive. Despite each company and system administrator using a specific policy for making and restoring backups, we should learn how to perform a simple restoration of a folder.

Time for action – restoring a backup folder

After creating a backup, it's time to restore it. We'll restore the `/tmp/backup` folder to `testbackup` inside your `home` folder.

1. Access the **Backup Tool** from the main menu.
2. Click on the **Restore files** button.
3. Select the **Directory** checkbox and choose the **backup** folder from the **tmp** directory. For the **Destination** menu option, you should select **testbackup** from your **home** folder. Click the **Forward** button when you're ready:

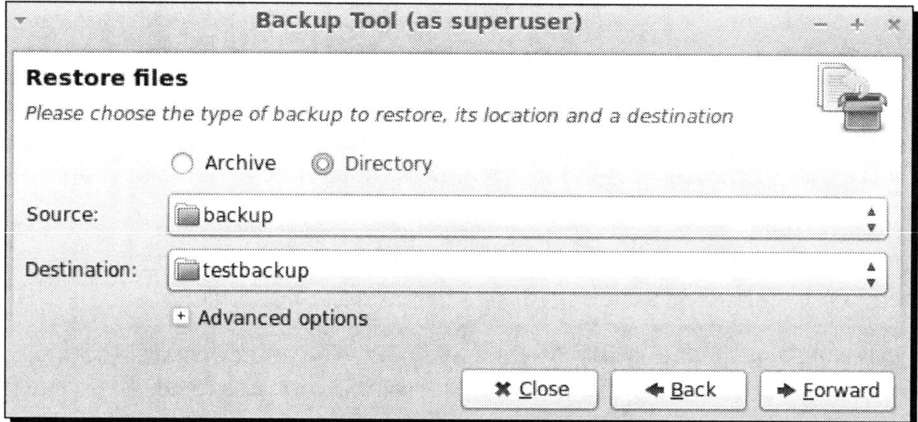

4. Review your options to make sure you're going to restore to the correct backup folder.
5. Click on **Apply,** and a new message will be displayed informing you about the restore operation. Your files should be available in the `testbackup` folder.

What just happened?

We've restored a backup inside the `home` folder. Obviously, the original backup should exist in the place where it was created previously. Thanks to this action, you can recover your files and folders without any problems.

Regarding **Advanced options**, when you're restoring a backup, you only can choose what kind of overwrite you want to apply. Some options are **never**, **by size**, **always**, and **checksum mismatch**; among these, one option is selected by default.

Alternative to restoring a directory, you can restore a backup file created using the same tool.

Have a go hero – create backup for applications

It would be interesting to prove how to create and restore a backup of some applications installed on your computer. You can do that using the **Backup software** selection and the **Restore software** selection buttons provided by Backup Tool.

Summary

Computer storage is complex as it's possible to find different kinds of devices and filesystems. Usually, technology used for storage is complicated and before taking a decision about what kind of storage and device of a filesystem should be used, it's important to make a complete analysis of the final scenario.

In this chapter, you've learned the basic concepts to deal with storage. Also, you know how to create and restore simple backups.

Specifically, we covered:

- Main filesystems used in Linux Mint and other GNU/Linux distributions
- How to assign disk quotas to users
- Graphically examining your disk usage
- How to create and make backups

In the next chapter, you're going to learn about security, which is one of the topics more relevant for system administrators.

9
Security

Security is without doubt one of the most important aspects for system administrators. In this chapter, we're going to learn about the basic mechanisms and tools that can be used to secure our Linux Mint computer.

In this chapter, we're going to cover the following topics:

- Running an SSH server
- Installing anti-virus software
- Installing and configuring a firewall
- Using a security module for the kernel
- Building a security checklist

Running an SSH server

Sometimes you need to establish a remote connection from your computer to a server. Also, users need access to your server or servers. A remote connection allows you to execute commands directly on the server from your computer. **Telnet** is one of the most used protocols to establish connections between computers. However, Telnet is not a secure protocol, so other protocols are needed when we need secure connections. Here is where **Secure Shell** (**SSH**) comes in. Thanks to SSH, users can connect securely to servers from their computers. From a technical point of view, SSH creates a secure channel between a server and a client. Usually, a client and server are different machines, but it's possible to use the same machine to play both roles.

Time for action – installing and configuring an SSH server

We're going to install and configure the **openssh-server** software to use our computer as an SSH server. Regarding configuration, our server will deny access to the root user, and it will be accessible through the `5656` port.

1. Click on the **Menu** button, and click again on the **Software Manager** button inside the **System** group.
2. Type `openssh server` in the text input field of the **Software Manager** application.
3. Select **openssh-server** and then click on the **Install** button.

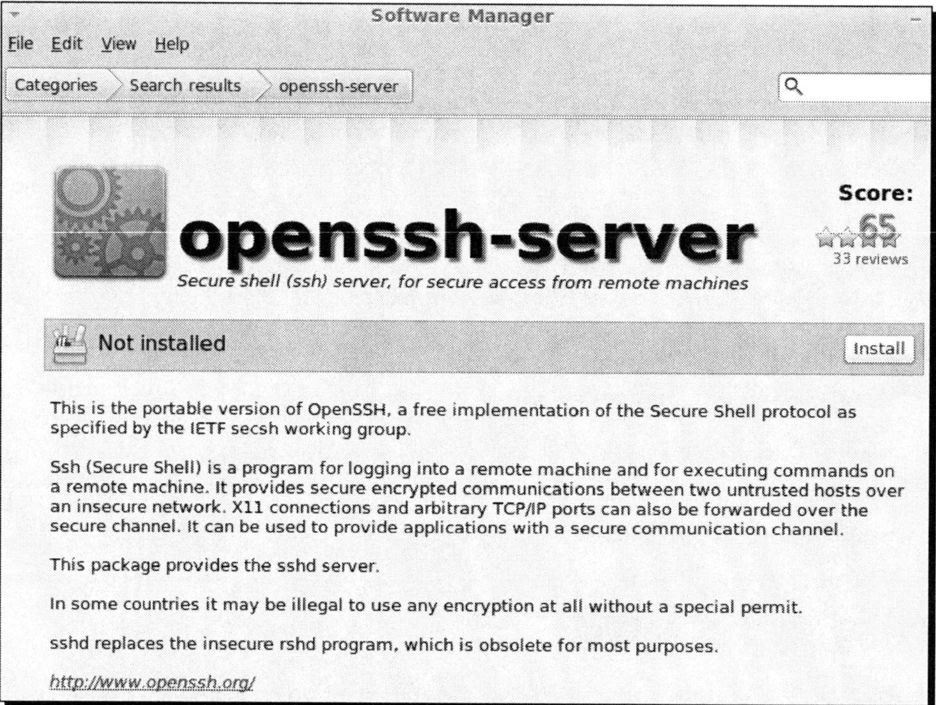

4. Now you have the **openssh-server** installed on you computer.
5. Launch MATE Terminal by clicking on the **Terminal** button accessible form the main menu.
6. We're going to edit a `/etc/ssh/sshd_config` file using the `vi` editor as the root user, so you should type the following command on the terminal:

```
$ sudo vi /etc/ssh/sshd_config
```

7. Type `i` to enter in edit mode inside `vi`. Look for a line that contains **PermitRootLogin** and replace it with the following line:

   ```
   PermitRootLogin no
   ```

8. Let's continue with the same file and look for another line that contains **Port** and replace that line with the following one:

   ```
   Port 5656
   ```

9. Save the `/etc/ssh/sshd_config` file; you can click the *Escape* key and then type `:wq`.

10. Now it's time to restart the SSH server. Then your server will be installed, configured, and ready to use. You can test this by executing the following command:

    ```
    $ sudo restart ssh
    ```

11. You can test your SSH server by trying to connect to it and typing on the terminal the following command:

    ```
    $ ssh localhost -p 5656
    ```

12. Now you will see a message asking for your authorization. Type `yes` and your password. You're now connected to your our server through the SSH protocol.

What just happened?

Thanks to the openssh-server software, we can create and configure an SSH server, which allows users to connect to a remote server through their computers. Linux Mint doesn't install the mentioned software by default, so you need to install it using **Software Manager** or the **Package Manager** application.

Once openssh-server is installed on your computer, users can connect to it directly using an SSH client. This kind of client is installed by default on major GNU/Linux distributions and Mac OS X computers.

Despite the openssh-server including a default configuration that allows us to connect to the server, it's recommended to change the configuration to suit our requirements. This is a task for system administrators. In our example, we don't allow connections through the root user, and we change the default `22` port to `5656`. These changes provide minimum security for SSH connections against potential attackers trying to use the default port to connect to servers using SSH protocol. Thanks to our change in configuration, we're establishing a first-level wall. On the other hand, if we allow the root user to connect to our SSH server, somebody can crack the connection and get root access to our server, which is not good.

In order to change the configuration file for the SSH server, we used the `vi` editor, which is installed in Linux Mint by default. This is a **modal** editor, and by typing `:wq`, we're saving and exiting. On the other hand, when you type `i`, `vi` enters the **insert** mode. Obviously, you can use other editors such as `Pluma` for editing the configuration file.

Finally, we restarted the SSH daemon using the `restart` command and passing `ssh` as an argument. We'll talk more about daemon services in the next chapter. At the moment, we only need to know that the `restart` command is used for restarting services.

Installing anti-virus software

Everybody knows that Windows operating systems need anti-virus software because it's very common that viruses infect the family of Microsoft operating systems. Though it's more difficult to find viruses affecting a GNU/Linux distribution, it is a good practice to install an anti-virus on our server. One of the most popular anti-viruses for Linux is **Clam-AV** (`http://www.clamav.net`), so we're going to learn how to install it on our server.

Time for action – installing the Clam-AV anti-virus

We'll install the Clam-AV anti-virus on our computer:

1. Click on the **Menu** button and click again on the **Software Manager** button inside the **System** group.
2. Type `clamav` in the input box of the main window of **Software Manager**.
3. Click on the first element of the results list.
4. Now you can click on the **Install** button, and type your password when required.

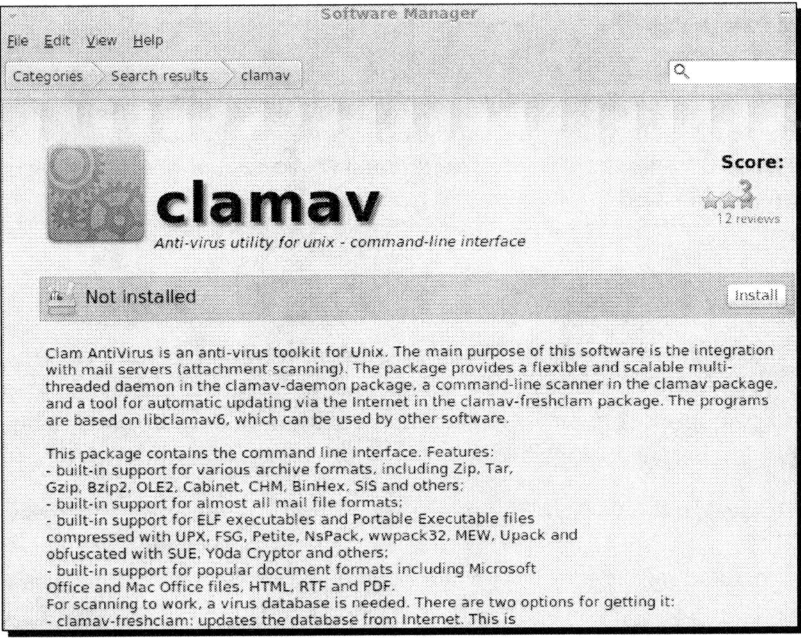

5. Once installation is finished, you can use the `clamscan` application from the command line.

6. In order to test our anti-virus, we're going to open the MATE Terminal and scan our `home` directory. You only need to type the following command:

   `$ clamscan`

7. The output of `clamscan` should be similar to the following screenshot:

```
arturo@han-solo ~ $ clamscan
/home/arturo/.profile: OK
/home/arturo/.gksu.lock: Empty file
/home/arturo/.Xauthority: OK
/home/arturo/.pulse-cookie: OK
/home/arturo/.vboxclient-display.pid: OK
/home/arturo/.bash_history: OK
/home/arturo/.xsession-errors: OK
/home/arturo/.vboxclient-seamless.pid: OK
/home/arturo/.ICEauthority: OK
/home/arturo/.dmrc: OK
/home/arturo/.bash_logout: OK
/home/arturo/.vboxclient-clipboard.pid: OK

----------- SCAN SUMMARY -----------
Known viruses: 1307463
Engine version: 0.97.3
Scanned directories: 1
Scanned files: 11
Infected files: 0
Data scanned: 0.00 MB
Data read: 0.00 MB (ratio 0.00:1)
Time: 7.618 sec (0 m 7 s)
```

What just happened?

We've used the **Software Manager** application for installing an application. In this case, we've installed Clam-AV anti-virus, which contains a main executable called `clamscan`. This command scans a directory and searches for viruses in our system. When the scan is finished, we get a simple report with information about scanned files and directories and which of them are infected.

Configuring a firewall

A **firewall** is one of the most important components in computer security. From the technical point of view, a firewall is a barrier designed to prevent unauthorized access to services and resources in a computer. Software and hardware components can be used to build a firewall. We're going to focus only on software.

The configuration of a firewall can be pretty easy or very complicated; depends on the security level that we want to apply. Obviously, it's different to configure a web server and a computer workstation. In order to use and configure a firewall in Linux, we can use a program called `iptables`, which is a packet filtering application based on rules defined by system administrators. Linux kernel uses different kernel modules to apply rules and creates a firewall for a computer.

Despite `iptables` being a very good application, it's not easy for beginners. This application doesn't use a graphical interface and it's *required* to know how to apply rules from the command line. However, Linux Mint includes a GUI application that provides a frontend to **Uncomplicated Firewall** (`ufw`), a piece of software designed to build firewalls easily. We'll now learn how to use this useful tool to configure a simple firewall.

Time for action – how to configure a simple firewall

As a simple example of building a firewall in Linux Mint, we're going to configure our firewall to deny access to a specific IP (`192.168.1.66`) to port `22`. Remember that we configured this port previously to run an SSH server.

1. Go to the main menu and click on the **Firewall Configuration** button belonging to the **Administration** category.
2. Then a new window will be displayed; click on the **Unlock** button and type your password.
3. Activate the firewall by selecting the **ON** option in **Status**.
4. Access the **Edit** menu and click on the **Add Rule...** button.

5. Click on the **Advanced** tab and select **Deny** for the first drop-down option. Then type `192.168.1.66` in the **From** input box and `22` for the port input box.

6. In the **To** input box, type your IP and type `22` again for the port. Click on the **Add** button when you're ready:

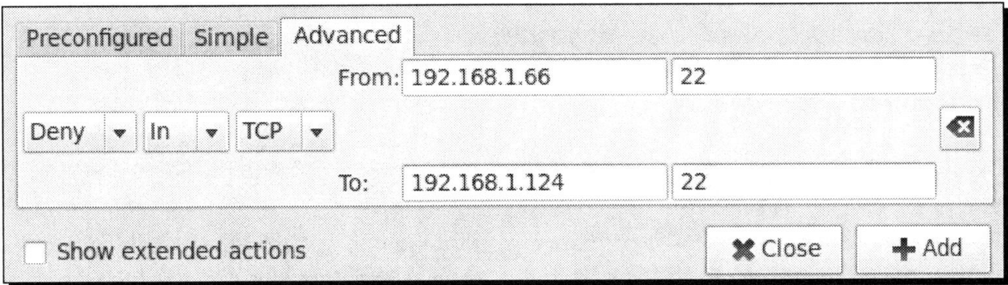

7. Then click the **Close** button and you'll see how your new rule has been added to the rules list:

8. Your firewall is configured and is now up and running.

What just happened?

Linux Mint allows us to configure and run a firewall through an application called `Gufw`. This tool is a simple and intuitive frontend to `ufw`, another tool for configuring a firewall, which is easier than `iptables`. `Gufw` has three main controls that allow us to enable or disable a firewall, and helps control incoming and outgoing traffic. A simple list shows us the rules that are enabled, and the two buttons below this list allows us to add and remove rules.

Keep in mind that the default behavior in `ufw` is to block all incoming traffic and allow outgoing traffic. Usually, system administrators prefer to block everything and then configure the applications, ports, and protocols that are allowed for connections. This technique is known as **white list**.

Basically, you can choose three actions that will be applied to incoming and outgoing traffic for your machine: **Allow**, **Deny**, and **Reject**. The difference between **Deny** and **Reject** actions is that the first one implies that each packet will be discarded. However, **Reject** means that server will send a response to the client informing about the computer using a firewall that denies access.

We've used advanced options to select IPs and ports, but also it's possible to use the **Preconfigured** and **Simple** tabs to allow or deny access only to applications and to protocols respectively.

Have a go hero – disabling firewall on startup using the command line

You've learned how to use `Gufw` to configure your firewall. In addition to this tool, you can use the `ufw` application directly from the command line. For example, you can disable your firewall on startup. In order to do that, launch the MATE Terminal and type the following command:

```
$ sudo ufw disable
```

After executing the preceding command, you'll receive a message such as the following:

```
Firewall stopped and disabled on system startup
```

Using a security module for the kernel

Linux kernel offers system administrators mechanisms to support control access policies to actions that applications can execute inside an operating system. Currently, **Security-Enhanced Linux** (**SELinux**) and **Application Armor** (**AppArmor**) are the most popular tools for that purpose. SELinux was developed by the United States **National Security Agency** (**NSA**), and it provides a set of Linux kernel modifications that can be applied to different GNU/Linux operating systems. The design and architecture of SELinux allow system administrators to create different policies that will be applied to users and processes running on the operating system. Related to SELinux, we find AppArmor, a security module designed for the Linux kernel. Thanks to this module, it's possible to establish a set of policies through different profiles to restrict what each program can do. If a program contains a security vulnerability, AppArmor can detect it leaving other software unaffected. In other words, AppArmor restricts capabilities of a program to apply a predefined security profile.

AppArmor and SELinux use **Linux Security Modules** (**LSM**), a framework for supporting different computer security models for the Linux kernel. Basically, LSM provides tools to implement mandatory access control based on different policies.

Linux Mint includes SELinux and AppArmor, but they aren't installed by default. AppArmor is easy to configure, deploy, and learn, so we'll find out how to install it on our server.

Time for action – installing AppArmor

The learning curve for AppArmor is hard, so we're only going to learn how to install it here:

1. Launch **Software Manager**.
2. Look for **apparmor**, select it from the list, and click on the **Install** button.

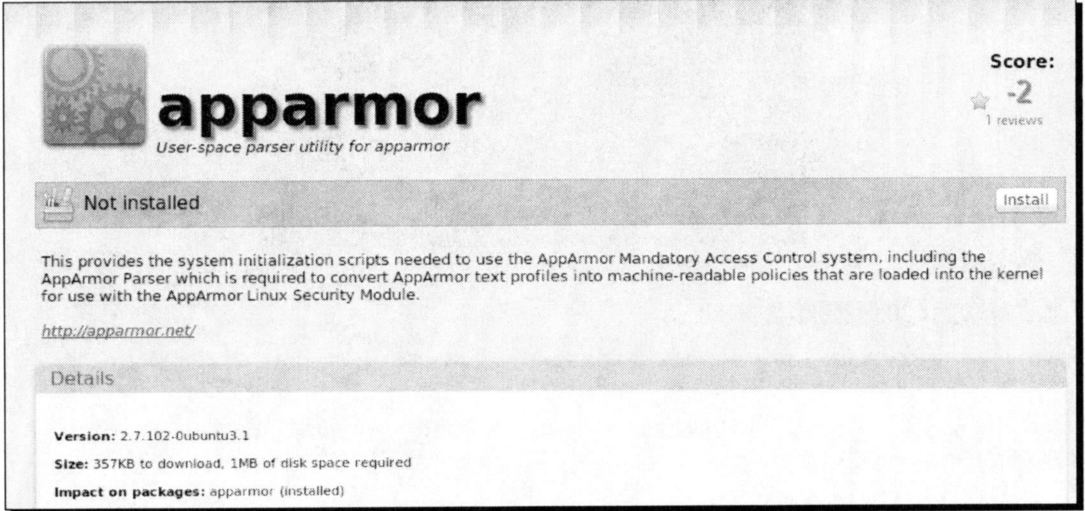

3. Once AppArmor is installed, you can check its status when executing the following command on MATE Terminal:

```
$ sudo apparmor_status
```

4. We'll see something like the following screenshot:

```
apparmor module is loaded.
You do not have enough privilege to read the profile set.
[arturo@hanlenovo ~]$ sudo apparmor_status
apparmor module is loaded.
18 profiles are loaded.
18 profiles are in enforce mode.
   /sbin/dhclient
   /usr/bin/evince
   /usr/bin/evince-previewer
   /usr/bin/evince-previewer//launchpad_integration
   /usr/bin/evince-previewer//sanitized_helper
   /usr/bin/evince-thumbnailer
   /usr/bin/evince-thumbnailer//sanitized_helper
   /usr/bin/evince//launchpad_integration
   /usr/bin/evince//sanitized_helper
   /usr/bin/freshclam
   /usr/lib/NetworkManager/nm-dhcp-client.action
   /usr/lib/connman/scripts/dhclient-script
   /usr/lib/cups/backend/cups-pdf
   /usr/lib/telepathy/mission-control-5
   /usr/lib/telepathy/telepathy-*
   /usr/sbin/cupsd
   /usr/sbin/mysqld
   /usr/sbin/tcpdump
0 profiles are in complain mode.
4 processes have profiles defined.
0 processes are in enforce mode.
0 processes are in complain mode.
4 processes are unconfined but have a profile defined.
   /sbin/dhclient (1739)
   /usr/bin/freshclam (1396)
   /usr/sbin/cupsd (784)
   /usr/sbin/mysqld (1069)
```

What just happened?

We simply installed AppArmor from the **Software Manager** application. The package included in Linux Mint provides different executable commands, such as `apparmor_status` and `apparmor_parser`. The first one offers us information about the defined and enabled profiles, and `apparmor_parser` is used for loading profiles into the Linux kernel.

If you're interested in learning more about how to configure AppArmor, you can take a look at the official documentation at `http://wiki.apparmor.net/index.php/Documentation`.

Managing your password safely

System administrators work with passwords each day. Connecting to servers, accessing resources, and managing users are actions that require the use of passwords. Storing passwords in a safe place is very important and it's critical for the security of systems. If we can use a tool to store, read, and update passwords, the daily job will be easier. One of the most popular software to carry out these tasks concerning passwords is **KeePass** (`http://keepass.info/`), a tool designed to manage passwords in a secure way. Basically, KeePass uses only a master password that the user should remember. This master password locks a database where other passwords are stored. From the technical point of view, KeePass uses two of the most secure encryption algorithms: **AES** and **Twofish**.

Time for action – installing and using KeePass

We'll learn how to install and use KeePass for storing some passwords. After installing KeePass, we'll create a new password for a user called `lucas`, who has access to a development server.

1. Go to the **Software Manager** application, look for **keepass2**, select the first item of searched items, and click on the **Install** button.
2. Once **KeePass2** is installed, you can launch it by accessing the main menu and by clicking on the **KeePass2** menu option belonging to the **Accessories** group.
3. Select the **File** option in the toolbar of the main window of **KeePass2** and click on the **New...** menu option.
4. Then a new window asking for the master password is displayed. We'll type the same password in the **Master password** and **Repeat password** input boxes.

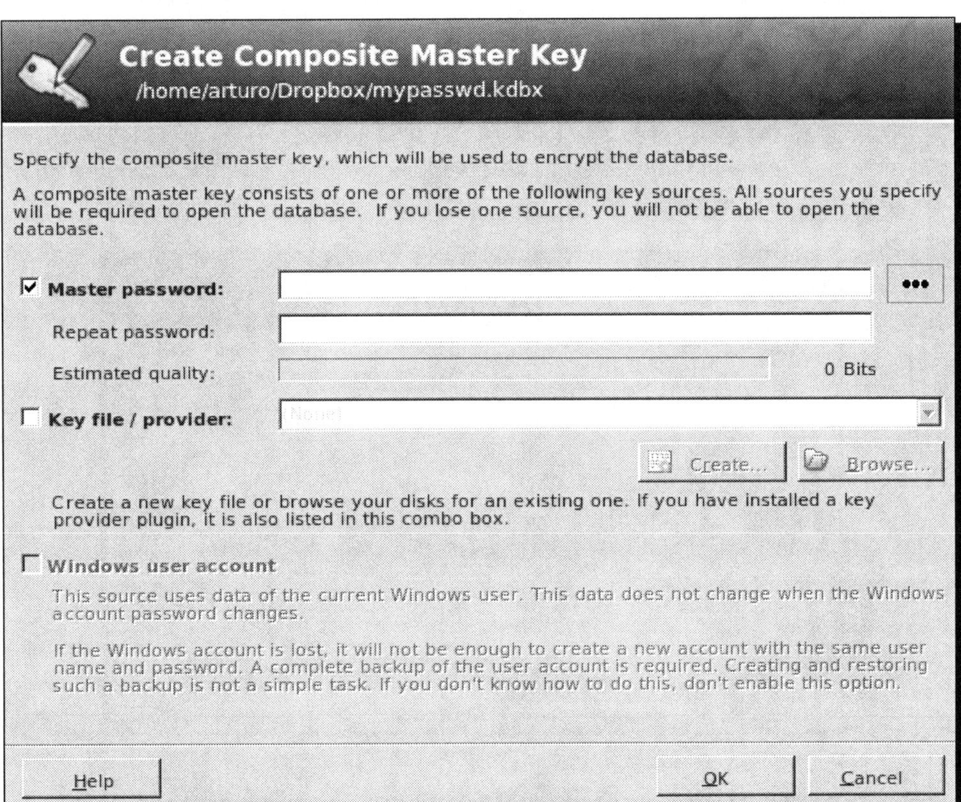

5. Click on **OK** when you're ready and a new dialog window will be displayed. Now, we need to choose a name for a database where passwords will be stored. Choose a name and a database description, then click on the **OK** button:

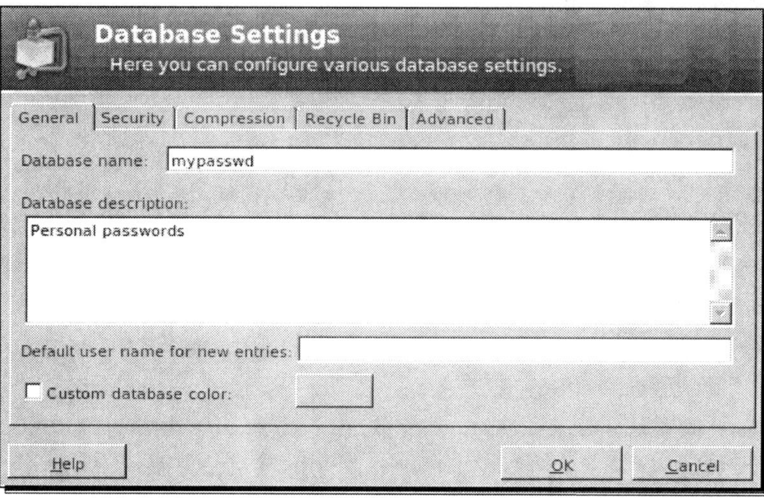

6. Your new database has been created and **KeePass** displays a tree widget where you can find different categories below the name of your database.

7. Now, go to the **Edit** menu and click on the **Add entry...** menu option. You will see a new dialog window. Enter a title and a username, and the password will be generated by default.

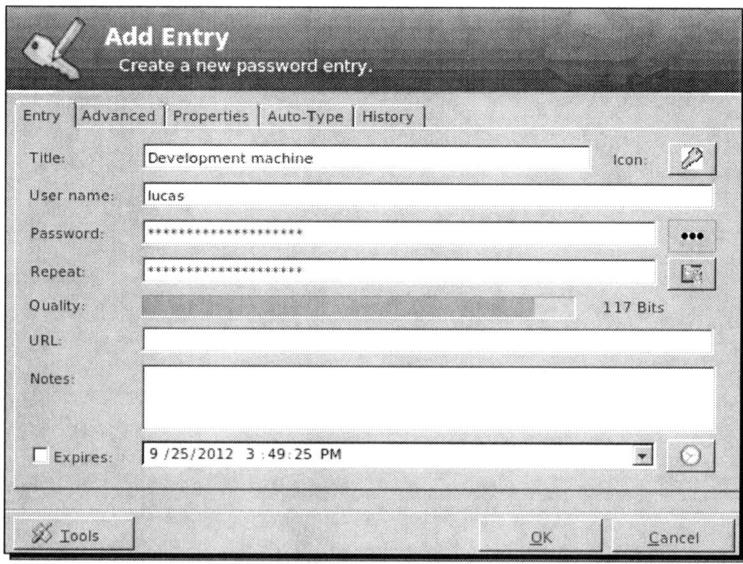

8. Click on the **OK** button, and a new entry will be created for your password.

What just happened?

KeePass is a complete tool to manage passwords. You can use and create many categories to organize your passwords. By default, passwords are generated when you create a new entry. It's possible to change configuration and decide how passwords are generated by default. Surely you must have realized that passwords are hidden, and you only can see stars. In order to change that, click on the button close to the **Password** input box.

Each time you access KeePass, you need to type your master password. However, when you click on an entry, you'll see information, including the password that you entered before.

Other useful functionality provided by KeePass is the ability to generate random passwords, although you don't want to use this tool to store it.

Building a security checklist

When the system administrator is configuring a safe server, it's a very good practice to use a simple checklist with some issues that should be checked. We're going to build one of these checklists based on concepts that we've learned in this chapter. Specifically, our checklist will contain the following issues:

- Install and enable only services that users need.
- Build and run a firewall based on a specific policy.
- Disable root access through SSH and change the default port for this connection service.
- Install and configure an anti-virus; Clam-AV is a good choice.
- Keep your system up-to-date. Always install security updates for your operating system and applications.
- Use KeePass or another password manager to store, read, and write your password securely.
- Choose secure passwords that include different types of characters.
- Encrypt your sensitive data. **GNU Privacy Guard** (**GPG**) can help you to do that. Also, Linux Mint allows you to encrypt your `home` folder from the installation process.
- If your computer needs extra security, it's a good idea to install and configure a network protocol analyzer such as **Wireshark**. In addition, you can install a network intrusion detection tool such as **Snort**.

Summary

In this chapter, we talked about security, one of the most important issues for system administrators. We looked at some tools such as KeePass, Clam-AV, AppArmor, and `Gufw`.

Specifically, we covered the following topics:

- Running an SSH server
- Installing Clam-AV anti-virus
- Installing and configuring a simple firewall using Gufw
- Discovering AppArmor and SELinux
- Installing and using KeePass for managing passwords
- Defining a security checklist

Despite having learned some basic tools to secure our computer, we can use other tools for the same purpose. For example, it's a good idea to use a tool to detect network intrusions. Inside this kind of software, Snort (`http://www.snort.org`) is one of the most popular. On the other hand, tools such as Wireshark (`http://www.wireshark.org`) can help you to analyze traffic in your network, which is very useful to detect potential security risks. After learning basic concepts and tools about security, you're ready to learn how to monitor your system, which will be explained in the next chapter.

10
Monitoring Your System

Once a computer is configured and different services are running, it's time to make sure everything is correct and things continue as usual. This chapter is going to introduce ways to monitor a system that is taking care of services and running processes, and how computer resources, such as memory, CPU, and network, are used.

In this chapter, we're going to cover the following topics:

- What are processes and services?
- Starting and stopping services
- Activating services
- Listing the running processes
- Displaying CPU, memory, and network usage

Processes and services

Novice Linux users always ask about two widely used concepts in GNU/Linux distributions: processes and services. These are very important for system administrators because they describe the applications that are running on our operating system. Obviously, we need to take care with that when we talk about how to supervise a computer system. The number of processes and services impact the performance of a server directly. System administrators should control which applications are running and how they are affecting the operating system and other resources and devices.

Basically, a **process** is a computer program or application in execution, including its current activity, that affects the resources such as CPU, open files, and memory. The operating system needs a set of information about each process in execution. This kind of information is known as **process descriptors** and includes state, parent processes, list of open files, memory address, and a unique identification number called PID.

We also found services related to processes. A **service** is a computer program that runs without direct intervention of an operating system user. It's very common to use the term "background" to refer to this kind of execution. Keep in mind that an application running in the background doesn't send any output to a terminal, though it is a common practice to use a file for this purpose. In UNIX and Linux-based operating systems, it's very usual to talk about **daemons** to refer to services. We can consider both concepts as equivalent. The Linux kernel starts some daemons at boot time, so the system administrator can decide about that. A simple convention is to use the suffix "d" to identify which programs are running as daemons. For example, `sshd` is the name of the daemon running an SSH server.

Usually, operating systems include tools to manage processes and services. Linux Mint is not an exception, and we'll find out later which tools can be used to manage running applications through services and processes.

In addition to processes and services, system administrators need to control and manage resources such as CPU, memory, network, and filesystems. All of them are part of system monitoring, because they affect the performance. In this chapter, we'll learn the basics about how to monitor our system, while taking care with mentioned resources including processes and services.

Starting and stopping services

System administrators need to know how to start and stop a specific service. As part of their daily job, system administrators check the running services and start new ones. Sometimes a service should be stopped; for example, when a service is no longer needed, we can stop it. Also, restarting can be required. All of these tasks can be carried out through an application called `initctl`. Let's see how to use it.

Time for action – stopping and starting an SSH daemon

We're going to learn how to stop and start our SSH service. Remember that we learned how to install an SSH previously in *Chapter 9, Security*. After installing this application, our SSH service will be running by default, so we'll now look at how to stop it.

1. Launch the MATE Terminal as usual.
2. Type the following command in the shell:

   ```
   $ sudo initctl stop ssh
   ```

3. Our SSH daemon is stopped and you'll receive an output message such as the following one:

   ```
   ssh stop/waiting
   ```

4. Now, we're going to launch our SSH daemon again. Just type the following command:

   ```
   $ sudo initctl start ssh
   ```

5. Once the SSH service starts running, you can see a message such as the following one:

   ```
   ssh start/running, process 2436
   ```

6. Also, you can find out the current status of the SSH service by executing the following command:

   ```
   $ sudo initctl status ssh
   ```

What just happened?

Linux Mint includes a tool called `initctl` that offers us control over the `init` daemon. This daemon is a special one, which gets started during the boot process of the Linux Kernel, and it's the parent of the rest of the services and processes. Usually, `init` has a PID of `1` and Linux Mint implements a specific event-based daemon called `Upstart`.

The `initctl` application accepts many commands as arguments; two of them are `start` and `stop` as you've learned already. As a third argument, we can pass the name of the service that will be affected by the operation, so the argument `stop ssh` indicates the operation and service name respectively.

In our example, we checked the current status of our SSH service using the `list` operation. This command returns a simple message informing us whether the service is up or down. Also, it's possible to use the `restart` operation, which stops and starts a specific server in that order.

It's important to know that we need to run `initctl` as the root user, otherwise we cannot start, stop, or restart services. The reason for this is that only the root user has access to these kind of operations. It doesn't make sense if any user can do that, because services are important for the security and the integrity of the system.

Have a go hero – checking current status of all services

Sometimes system administrators need to know about the current status of all running and stopped services in the operating system. In order to do that, we can use the `initctl` tool passing an argument called `list`. The command is as follows:

```
$ sudo initctl list
```

We'll get a response, as shown in the following screenshot:

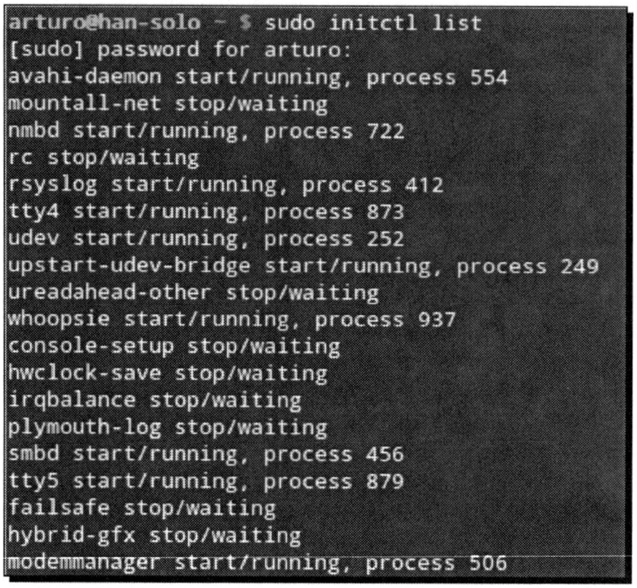

```
arturo@han-solo ~ $ sudo initctl list
[sudo] password for arturo:
avahi-daemon start/running, process 554
mountall-net stop/waiting
nmbd start/running, process 722
rc stop/waiting
rsyslog start/running, process 412
tty4 start/running, process 873
udev start/running, process 252
upstart-udev-bridge start/running, process 249
ureadahead-other stop/waiting
whoopsie start/running, process 937
console-setup stop/waiting
hwclock-save stop/waiting
irqbalance stop/waiting
plymouth-log stop/waiting
smbd start/running, process 456
tty5 start/running, process 879
failsafe stop/waiting
hybrid-gfx stop/waiting
modemmanager start/running, process 506
```

Activating services

Previously we've learned how to start and stop services through the command line. However, Linux Mint also includes a simple GUI application that allows us, with a simple button click, to select the services we want to activate or deactivate when the system starts. Let's see how to activate services through the **Services Settings** application.

Time for action – activating Samba

In order to share files and directories with Windows systems, we can use the **Samba** protocol. Let's imagine that we have installed in our Linux Mint a set of tools and a daemon to do that. We're going to learn how to activate a Samba service.

1. Click on the **Menu** button and click again on the **All Applications** button.
2. Click on the **Services** menu option of the **Administration** group.
3. A new window belonging to the **Service Settings** application is displayed.
4. Look for the **samba** option and click on it:

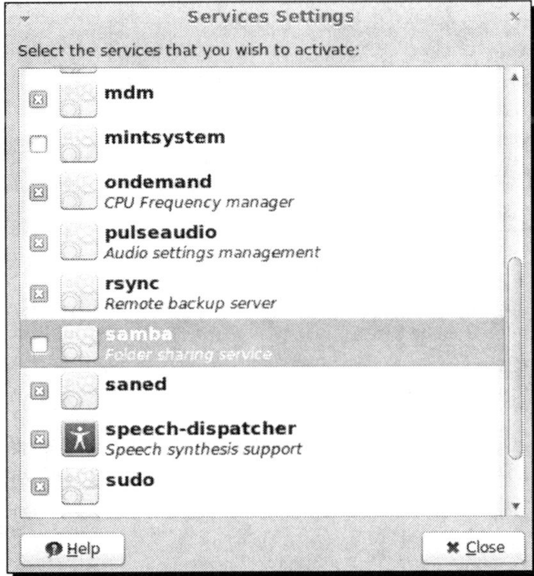

5. After selecting the **samba** option, you must type your password. Then click on the **Close** button. Next time you boot your system, the Samba service will be started automatically.

What just happened?

Usually, it's very useful to configure many services to start automatically at boot time. By applying this configuration, the system administrator can save time and they are sure that services will start automatically.

Despite configuring your services through the command line, Linux Mint provides a simple and intuitive tool to do that. As you have learned, this tool is **Services Settings,** and you can access it easily from the main menu.

Listing the running processes

One of the most important things that the system administrator should supervise is the list of current processes running on the operating system of each machine under their control. Remember that each running process is using some resource, such as the CPU, memory, and files. This means that it's important to control processes because they affect the performance and security of the system directly.

Linux Mint offers us a specific tool for monitoring processes, CPU, memory, network, and the filesystem of our machine. We're going to learn how to use this tool for monitoring our system, and we'll learn about how to list the running processes.

Time for action – list the processes running on our machine

Earlier we talked about a tool for monitoring our system—**System Monitor**. It is installed in Linux Mint by default. Let's learn how to access this tool and how to list the running processes.

1. Click on the **Menu** button and click again on the **System Monitor** button:

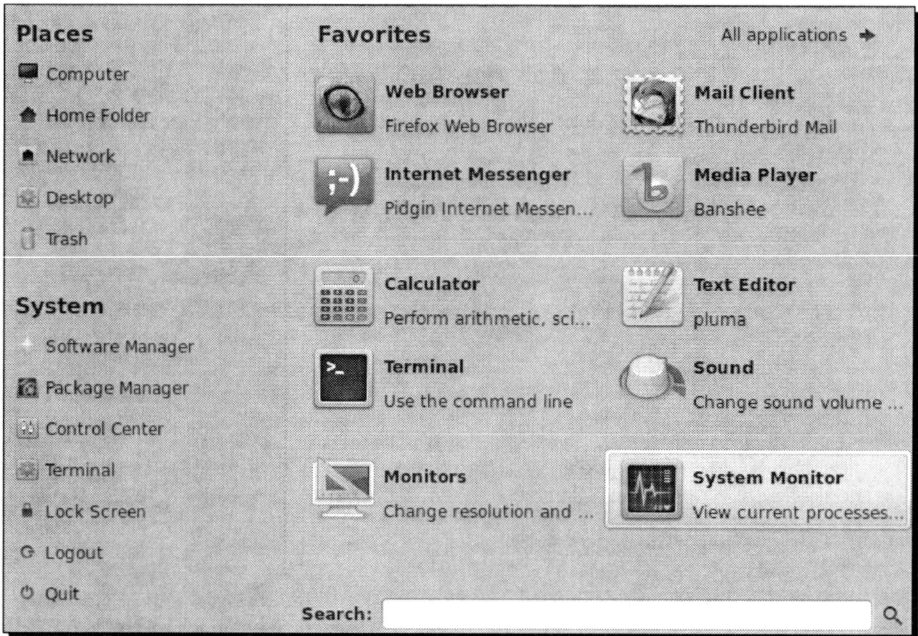

2. Then a new window is displayed. Click on the **Processes** tab.
3. Now, you can see the processes that are running and additional information about them, such as CPU and memory usage:

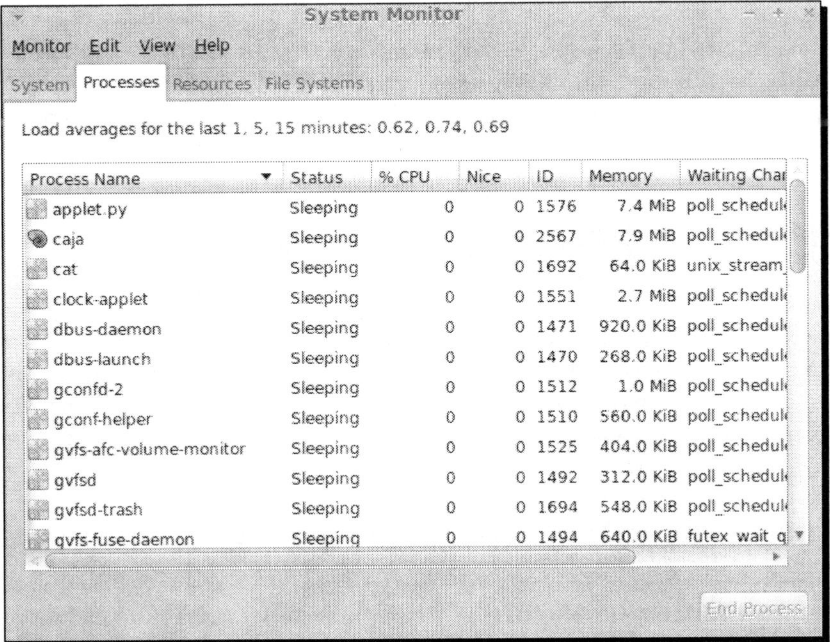

What just happened?

Thanks to the **System Monitor** tool, you can see which processes are running, and you can find out their current status and the CPU and the memory usage of each one. In addition to this kind of information, **System Monitor** displays the load average of the computer based on the CPU usage. As you can observe, **System Monitor** displays information about the load average for the last one, five, and fifteen minutes. These values help the system administrator to control the current status of a machine, and threshold values can be applied to decide when some actions should be taken. Remember that our goal is to help our machine to run processes without collapsing the system.

System Monitor offers us menu options to display different views about running processes. Specifically, we can display all processes (default view), active processes, and my processes (root user by default). Also, it's possible to change the order of displaying information, so you can display, for example, all processes ordered according to their memory consumption.

The **Edit** menu gives us access to different actions that can be applied to a running process. You can stop, kill, and change the priority of each process. In order to take these actions, first you need to select a specific process from the list. Then you can execute each action by accessing the options belonging to the mentioned **Edit** menu.

Another interesting feature provided by **System Monitor** is the possibility of finding out which files are opened by each process. You only need to select a process and then click on the **Open Files** menu option of the **Edit** menu. Keep in mind that this information can change automatically when the window is open, as each process can open and close files during its execution.

Displaying CPU, memory, and network usage

Besides processes and services, it's very important to take care of resources on our machine as applications need to use these resources. CPU, memory, and network are the most important resources used by our computer, so the system administrator should always keep an eye on them. To make life easier, Linux Mint provides information about how these resources are used in real time through the **System Monitor** application. We'll learn how to display the current use of these resources.

Time for action – Displaying resources information in real time

Let's find out how to get basic information about main computer resources that are used in real time:

1. Click on the **Menu** button and click again on the **System Monitor** button.
2. Click on the **Resources** tab and you have access to all information regarding CPU, memory, and network usage as shown:

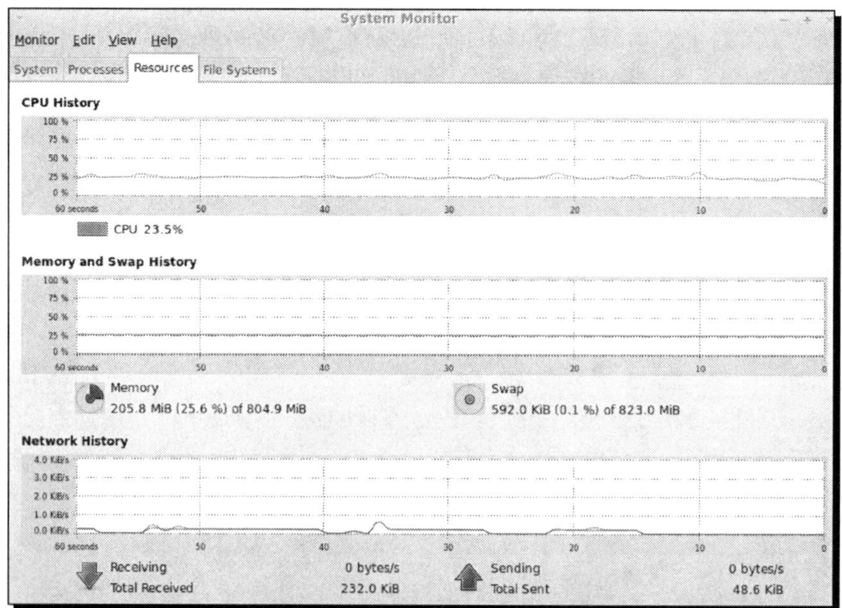

What just happened?

When you click on the **Resources** tab of **System Monitor**, a set of charts is displayed. The first one offers you information about the percentage of CPU usage by time. Also, the current percentage of CPU is displayed below the chart.

Regarding memory, we find information related to the main and swap memory usage. Percentage values related to the total memory are displayed. The purple line on the chart represents main memory, and the green line is used for the swap memory. Both lines are displayed inside the chart so you can compare both easily.

Network information is separated between received and sent packages; different colors are used to denote them. You can see total packages in bytes that have been sent and received by your computer. Also, you can obtain how many of them were sent or received each second.

As you will have realized, all information about resources is displayed based on history. This means that each graph is based on time, and it's alive in a sense that the information is displayed in real time.

Have a go hero – getting information about filesystems usage

In addition to memory, processes, CPU, and network usage, you can get information about your filesystem's usage. In order to take this action, you only need to click on the **File Systems** tab and **System Monitor** displays for each filesystem, information about mounted directories, total space, available space, and percentage of used space.

Summary

In this chapter, we've learned the basics about system monitoring, being an important area for system administrators. We introduced processes and services, and then we learned how to manage services and how to monitor the most valuable resources in a computer: memory, CPU, hard disks, and network.

Specifically, we covered the following:

- Basic concepts such as processes and services
- How to deal with services
- Finding out the running processes and being able to stop them
- Charts indicating how the usage of CPU, memory, and networking are affecting our computer

It's important to keep in mind that this chapter is just a basic introduction to system monitoring. This is a big area, and a good understanding and good practice requires experience, and it depends on the complexity of the system that we want to supervise.

At this point we know how to configure and supervise our computer; in the next chapter, we're going to talk about how to solve common problems that can happen when a Linux Mint server or workstation is running.

11
Troubleshooting

Sooner or later system administrators will face problems that affect computers. Sometimes these problems will be related to hardware, and other times to software. It's very important to know which tools we can use to identify problems and try to solve them. In this chapter, we'll learn basic commands and tools that can help us determine what is happening with the network, hardware, kernel, processes, and filesystems.

In this chapter we shall learn the following topics:

- Hardware
- Checking log files
- Kernel
- Networking
- Processes and filesystems

Hardware

A lot of the time, users detect small problems related to hardware and system administrators can solve them quickly. However, sometimes a problem can be difficult to detect and solve. Also, many devices or resources can trigger more than one problem.

Memory and CPU are very important hardware components for our computer. We need to take care of them because a high load can block the operating system. Also, PCI and USB devices can stop working properly, so we should check them when we detect hardware problems.

Time for action – checking memory, CPU, USB, and PCI devices

In Linux Mint, we can find tools and commands that can help us to find out what is happening with our hardware. Let's look at some commands to check the memory, CPU, and USB, PCI devices.

1. Our first goal will be to get information about all USB devices installed on our computer. Open MATE Terminal as usual, and type the following command:

   ```
   $ lsusb
   ```

2. Now, it's the turn for PCI devices, so we're going to execute the next command:

   ```
   $ lspci
   ```

3. The output of the previous command will show you something similar to the following screenshot:

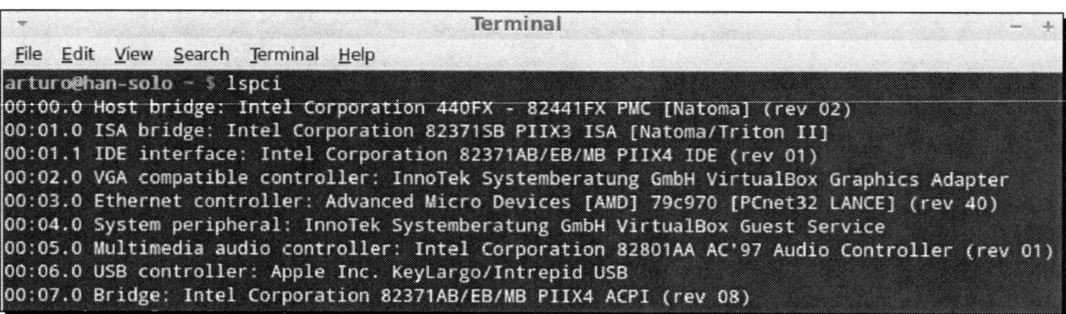

4. A complete and detailed list of all our hardware can be obtained by executing the following command:

   ```
   $ sudo lshw
   ```

5. In order to get information about memory, we'll execute the following command:

   ```
   $ cat /etc/meminfo
   ```

6. As the output, we'll get some lines like the following:

   ```
   MemTotal:       824188 kB
   MemFree:        285016 kB
   Buffers:         64228 kB
   ```

7. Regarding our CPU, we can launch the following command to get information about processors installed on our machine:

   ```
   $ cat /etc/cpuinfo
   ```

What just happened?

In order to get a complete list with a lot of information about our PCI and USB devices, we can execute the `lspci` and `lusb` commands respectively. These commands help us to know if devices are recognized by our computer or not. Keep in mind that some devices cannot be detected by the operating system; in that case we need to solve the problem.

On the other hand, `/proc/cpu` is a file that contains information about the CPU installed on a computer. The `cat` command has been used for displaying content of the mentioned file. Regarding the `/proc/cpu` file, we find the `/proc/meminfo` file, which contains data about memory used in our computer. Some information offered by the mentioned file includes total memory size and how much memory is available.

The `lshw` command means "list hardware" and it shows us an exhaustive list of all hardware installed on a computer. Don't forget to execute the `lshw` command as the root user.

Checking log files

Linux Mint uses a set of files for logging different activities happening in the operating system. This kind of information includes data about how resources, such as files or network are used. All of these files reside inside the `/var/log/` directory. Only the root user can change these files, but other users can read it. One of most important log files is `/var/log/syslog`, which is a generic log where different applications write data about its activity. In addition to this generic log file, we can find a lot of them such as `Xorg.0.log`, `dmesg`, `kern.log`, and `dpkg.log`. Usually, specific applications such as MySQL and Apache, use their own log files inside the `/var/log/` directory. It's a good practice to check the log directory to find out what's happening on our computer.

Time for action – listing the last five lines of the syslog file

We're going to check the last five lines of our `syslog` file using the `tail` command:

1. Open the MATE Terminal as usual.
2. Execute the following command:

   ```
   $ tail -5 /var/log/syslog
   ```

3. As the output, you'll get some lines informing you about the last actions saved in `syslog` file.

What just happened?

We used a command called `tail` to read the last lines of our `syslog` file. This command reads a file in reverse order and can receive a number as an argument. This number is used to display a specific number of lines of the file. Obviously, you can read the `syslog` file using your favorite editor, but it's easier to use `tail` as the output of this command is sent directly to your terminal.

Kernel

The Linux kernel is the most important component of our Linux Mint operating system so we need to take care of it, and we should check if it's working properly. The Linux kernel uses **modules**, which are components that implement and extend the functionality of the kernel, and that can be loaded or unloaded into the kernel on demand without rebooting.

The use of modules has a lot of advantages; one of them is that we can save memory by loading only the required modules. Another clear advantage is the option of loading modules on the fly without rebooting your computer. It saves a lot of time, and we don't need to stop the service. Due to the importance of modules, system administrators should check the kernel and module status. We can do that, thanks to commands that we'll learn to use later.

Time for action – using lsmod, modprobe, and dmesg commands

System administrators can use some commands such as `lsmod`, `modprobe`, and `dmesg` to get information about the kernel. Let's discover how to use these commands.

1. Launch the MATE Terminal application.
2. Execute the following command:

   ```
   $ lsmod
   ```

3. The output of the previous command will display information about your loaded kernel modules.
4. We're going to execute the following command to get a list of all modules that can be loaded in the kernel:

   ```
   $ modprobe -l
   ```

5. Then it's time to execute the `dmesg` command, which will launch a lot of messages, so we'll use it less to control output. Type the next command in your terminal:

   ```
   $ dmesg | more
   ```

What just happened?

In order to know the status of each module loaded by the Linux kernel, we can execute the `lsmod` command. From the technical point of view, this command only formats the content of the `/proc/modules` file.

System administrators need to know how to load and unload modules in the Linux kernel. The `modprobe` command allows us to perform these actions. It receives as parameter the name of the module that will be loaded or unloaded. Passing the `-l` argument, we can find out which modules are available to load.

Finally, the `dmesg` command is very useful to get information related to kernel operations. For example, if we plug a USB device to our computer, the kernel will create a log message that can be read using the `dmesg` command. Thanks to the `more` command, you can read lines easier. Sure, You'll have realized that we used a pipe to send the output of `dmesg` to the input of `more`.

Networking

Nowadays, a network is one of the most valuable resources used by computers. It's hard to imagine a company without the Internet or a local network connection. Sometimes system administrators need to deal with problems related to networks, so it's very interesting to know which tools can be used to detect and solve common problems.

You will have heard about `ping`, a command to send information to computers and devices such as printers with the goal of getting a response and also making sure they're working properly. This command is very useful to check network connections; if `ping` doesn't get a response, the connection cannot be established, and something with a device or computer is failing the network communication. Related to `ping`, we find `route`, a command that shows the IP routing table of our computer. Also, `route` allows us to change that table. It's not possible to establish a connection outside our route table, so it's important to check it out when connections are failing.

Another useful command to get information about our network interfaces is `ifconfig`. For example, using `ifconfig` we can find out which IP is using each network interface of our server. Also, `ifconfig` allows us to configure network interfaces through the command line.

Linux Mint also includes `netstat`, a command that offers information about network connections, routing tables, interface statistics, masquerade connections, and multicast memberships. We'll learn more about the `netstat` command later.

Time for action – checking who is listening on what port

We're going to discover how to use the `netstat` command to find out what applications are listening on what ports:

1. Open MATE Terminal as usual.
2. Type and execute the following command:

```
$ netstat -tln
```

What just happened?

Despite executing `netstat` only to find out what programs are listening on what ports, this command can be used to get more information about our network connections and usage. If you execute `netstat` without any argument, you'll get information about all open sockets on your computer. Basically, `netstat` can be used for checking and monitoring all network activity on your computer. You can get more information about the `netstat` command through the `man` and `info` commands.

Processes and filesystems

Processes and filesystems cause many computer problems. Remember that processes are created by programs that reside in filesystems, so both of them are closely related. If something goes wrong with a computer, it's a good idea to take a look at which processes are running and how is the status of filesystems associated to these processes.

The `fuser` command is very useful, because it offers a list that shows what files are used for what process. Basically, we only need to execute this command by passing the name of a specific process as an argument.

Linux Mint and other GNU/Linux distributions include `strace`, a tool that can be employed to discover what system calls and libraries are used by a specific process. You can type `strace` followed by a command or application that you want to trace.

Usually, system administrators work with `top`, a command offering complete information about running processes, including data about CPU and memory consumption. Another useful tool to deal with processes is `ps`. We'll learn how to find a specific process using that command.

When system administrators need to take a quick look at the filesystem attached to a specific computer, they work with the `df` command, which provides information about the filesystem disk space usage. By passing the `-h` argument, we'll get a list with size, available and used space, percentage of usage, and the location where each filesystem is mounted. Many problems happen when filesystems are without space or aren't mounted, so it's a good idea to use `df` to detect these kinds of issues.

Time for action – finding a specific process

You're going to learn how to use the `ps` command to find information about a specific process running on your computer. In our case, we'll look for the SSH server daemon process.

1. Launch the MATE Terminal.
2. Type the following command in your shell:

   ```
   $ ps -ef | fgrep -i sshd
   ```

3. As a result of the last executed command, we'll get the following response:

   ```
   root         768       1  0        09:06     ?              00:00:00  /
   usr/sbin/sshd -D
   arturo    16017 10434  0 16:07 pts/3     00:00:00   fgrep -i sshd
   ```

What just happened?

As you've observed, we used the `ps` and `fgrep` commands together through a pipe connector. The `frep` command looks for a specific pattern, in our case `sshd` works as that pattern. The `ef` parameters indicate that we're looking at all running processes, using the output formatted according to the default values of the `ps` command. Using pipes we can redirect the output of the `ps` command to `fgrep`.

For sure you might be wondering why we got two lines if we only have just a single `sshd` process running. The answer is easy to explain: `sshd` string is another name for the piped command `fgrep`, so its output is also shown.

Each output line of `ps` offers us information about the process owner, path to the running process, PID (process ID), terminal associated, and time when it started. Keep in mind, that we got a question mark for the `sshd` process because it's a daemon not associated with any terminal.

If you need to kill a process or get more information about it, you can use the System Monitor tool included in Linux Mint. More information about this tool can be found in *Chapter 10, Monitoring*.

Summary

In this chapter, you've learned which tools and commands can help system administrators to detect and solve common problems related to hardware, network, kernel, filesystems, and processes. Despite each problem being unique, tools described in this chapter are very useful to check if different resources and devices are working properly.

Specifically, we covered:

- Checking hardware components such as memory, CPU, USB, and PCI devices
- Checking log files
- Learning about how to list loaded modules in the kernel
- Useful tools to check network connection and finding out what processes are listening on what ports
- Dealing with running processes

If you need to look for help to specific problems, the following resources can be very useful:

- Wiki with complete information for system administrators available at `http://sysadmin.wikia.com/wiki/Main_Page`.
- The Linux Documentation project offers a good collection of how to documents and guides available at:
    - `http://tldp.org/docs.html#howto`
    - `http://tldp.org/guides.html`
- The official Linux Mint documentation available at `http://www.linuxmint.com/documentation.php`
- The official Linux kernel documentation available at `http://kernel.org/doc/`

At this point, you've learned basic things about system administration in Linux Mint. Throughout this book we explained how to deal with user accounts, how to install and configure software, basic things about networking and security, how to create and restore backups, and the last chapter was dedicated to system monitoring. Finally, we finish by learning about tools and commands that can help us to face common and daily issues.

Index

Symbols

D

E

F

G

T

U

W

X

Thank you for buying
Linux Mint System Administration Beginner's Guide

About Packt Publishing

Packt, pronounced 'packed', published its first book "*Mastering phpMyAdmin for Effective MySQL Management*" in April 2004 and subsequently continued to specialize in publishing highly focused books on specific technologies and solutions.

Our books and publications share the experiences of your fellow IT professionals in adapting and customizing today's systems, applications, and frameworks. Our solution based books give you the knowledge and power to customize the software and technologies you're using to get the job done. Packt books are more specific and less general than the IT books you have seen in the past. Our unique business model allows us to bring you more focused information, giving you more of what you need to know, and less of what you don't.

Packt is a modern, yet unique publishing company, which focuses on producing quality, cutting-edge books for communities of developers, administrators, and newbies alike. For more information, please visit our website: `www.packtpub.com`.

About Packt Open Source

In 2010, Packt launched two new brands, Packt Open Source and Packt Enterprise, in order to continue its focus on specialization. This book is part of the Packt Open Source brand, home to books published on software built around Open Source licences, and offering information to anybody from advanced developers to budding web designers. The Open Source brand also runs Packt's Open Source Royalty Scheme, by which Packt gives a royalty to each Open Source project about whose software a book is sold.

Writing for Packt

We welcome all inquiries from people who are interested in authoring. Book proposals should be sent to author@packtpub.com. If your book idea is still at an early stage and you would like to discuss it first before writing a formal book proposal, contact us; one of our commissioning editors will get in touch with you.

We're not just looking for published authors; if you have strong technical skills but no writing experience, our experienced editors can help you develop a writing career, or simply get some additional reward for your expertise.

Koha 3 library Management System

ISBN: 978-1-849510-82-0 Paperback: 288 pages

Install, confi gure, and maintain your Koha installation with this easy-to-follow guide

1. A self-sufficient guide to installing and configuring Koha
2. Take control of your libraries with Koha library management system
3. Get a clear understanding of software maintenance, customization, and other advanced topics such as LDAP and Internationalization

---

CentOS 6 Linux Server Cookbook

ISBN: 978-1-849519-02-1 Paperback: 350 pages

Learn to comfigure Linux CentOS for the service you need; Providing Web services, FTP Services, and Mail Services

1. Quickly get CentOS up and running while customizing your installation with a few 'tricks of the trade'
2. Establish the basic needs of your server before building on that to achieve your goals
3. Practical and concise recipes lead you through what you need to manage the system, packages, file systems, and more

Please check **www.PacktPub.com** for information on our titles

CPSIA information can be obtained at www.ICGtesting.com
Printed in the USA
BVOW06s1547270713

327120BV00003B/116/P